Indians in Post-Apartheid South Africa

About the Author

Anand Singh, a South African of Indian descent, is presently Professor in Anthropology at the School of Anthropology, Gender and Historical Studies, University of KwaZulu-Natal, Durban. He did his MA in Social Anthropology from the University of Cape Town. In 1983, he won the Nelson Mandela Scholarship to the London School of Economics and Political Science, and completed an MSc in Social Policy and Administration in 1984. After joining the University of Durban-Westville (now part of the University of KwaZulu-Natal) in 1986 as a lecturer, he made the study of people of Indian origin his priority in research and has published numerous papers about them.

Indians in Post-Apartheid South Africa

Dr. ANAND SINGH

CONCEPT PUBLISHING COMPANY, NEW DELHI-110059

Cataloging in Publication Data—DK
Courtesy: D.K. Agencies (P) Ltd. <docinfo@dkagencies.com>

Singh, Anand.
Indians in post-apartheid South Africa / Anand Singh.
p. cm.
Includes bibliographical references (p.)
Includes index.
ISBN 8180692264

1. East Indians—South Africa—Social conditions. 2. East Indians South Africa—Economic conditions. 3. South Africa—Politics and government—1994- 4. South Africa—Race relations. I. Title.

DDC 305.891 406 8 21

ISBN-81-8069-226-4

First Published 2005

Published and Printed by
Ashok Kumar Mittal
Concept Publishing Company,
A/15-16, Commercial Block, Mohan Garden,
New Delhi-110059 (INDIA)

Phones : 25351460, 25351794
Fax : 091-11-25357103
Email : publishing@conceptpub.com

PREFACE

There are at least two issues that prompted me to research prevalent issues in Durban that are discussed in this book. Some time in 1986, while I was in the company of a man we all considered to be a spiritually enlightened soul and in whose presence the thoughts about class, race and religious background did not really matter. I was asked by him to be part of an envisaged school children's feeding scheme. In my haste to respond positively, I unthinkingly stated: "Yes I would not mind that. The African children are really starving in the townships! (low cost municipality housing)." He replied: "Yes, I know son. But you cannot get there just yet because of the political violence. So we will leave that out until it is safe to go there. But do you know how much the Indian children are also suffering in their townships?" I was dumbfounded for a while and used the feeble excuse that I was a student in Cape Town for almost three years, went on scholarship to London for a year and then returned to work in Cape Town for another year. Although I tried to justify this with conviction, I realized that I was not convinced by this myself. Coming from a middle-class background, I had to admit to myself that I knew very little about the extent of poverty in the Indian population in Durban, as well as about the history and state of the Indian population in South Africa. I eventually conceded ignorance to those around me about poverty among Indians in their working class townships that were built by the Durban Municipality and agreed to serve there through the feeding scheme.

Another realization that dawned upon me then was the academic and media focus on the marginality and poverty among Africans. It had acquired such currency amidst the political turmoil of the mid-1980s and early 1990s, that social science and humanities scholars barged en-masse into research and writing on African poverty. Clearly, over time, researching problems in African communities became almost the only politically correct thing to do, especially since generous research funding was being made available for it. It was also clear that apartheid was bursting at the seams and ready to meet its demise at any time. The preparation for a post-apartheid era attracted even the most conservative academics that swiftly changed, coats to capitalize on the abundance of research funding. 1 felt disinclined to move with such a flow and the urge to learn more about the community that 1 came from brought me to succumb to the desire to engage in research on people of Indian origin. I quietly went about reading the more critical accounts on South African Indian history, about which the strategists of apartheid would have preferred us remaining ignorant. At about the same time, i.e. since the early 1990s, a member of the executive of the Anthropology Association of Southern Africa (now Anthropology Southern Africa), urged members to "study up" or "study within" — with the intention to promote insider based research.

Fed up with the behaviour of opportunistic academics and feeling inadequate by my own new-found ignorance, 1 found this avenue attractive and decided to make people of Indian origin my focus for future research. This proved to be richly rewarding, especially since people whom I wished to write about often took me to be "one of them", by virtue of my own descent, and often spoke spontaneously because of this. It provided opportunities for collating data that 1 did not enjoy while studying people who were not of the racial and ethnic background into which apartheid classified me. The point of entry into 'outsider' communities is usually time-consuming and it is difficult to acquire levels of trust that might be sought as an insider. Very often, what first began as attendance at social gatherings, actually turned out to become important ethnographic data gathering exercises. It was in such gatherings that the transformation from euphoria to despondency was first noted, which was often supported by casual chat about the problems of informal settlements, the business opportunities that this gave rise to, and the ongoing problems between Indian bus owners and African taxi owners, the alleged deterioration in education and the increased want by youngsters to work overseas, or of families to emigrate in order to escape what they saw as a deteriorating political situation. Each one of these aspects tended to prevail in most social gatherings, around dinner tables and in casual conversations in numerous types of settings. The frequency of such conversations urged follow-ups on each issue and eventually provided enough material to constitute a chapter for this book. While the prevalent negativity in each chapter might imply a subversion of the positive spin-offs derived from the demise of apartheid, it is really intended to capture the political psyche of what I believe to be a large segment of the people of Indian origin at a particular historical juncture in South Africa. Such thoughts and perceptions should be useful to gauge the political climate of the country and the possible scenarios that lie ahead.

December 2004

Anand Singh
Westville Campus
University of KwaZulu-Natal

ACKNOWLEDGEMENTS

The University of Durban-Westville has been instrumental in supporting this project through financial aid, equipment and facilities. Without their support, this project is unlikely to have been completed in the time that it was. I would also like to thank my colleague and friend Dr. Alan Thorold for his advice, support and encouragement throughout this project, and Reshma Sathipersadh for proof-reading the initial drafts. I bear personal responsibility for errors that remain, including those in the typing.

CONTENTS

CHAPTER ONE

Introduction

This book is about people of Indian origin in post-apartheid South Africa. Its focus is on issues of historical and contemporary interest, especially within the population in several of the city of Durban's predominantly Indian suburbs. The work should be viewed in the context of the particular historical circumstances that have prevailed prior to the country's first democratic general election on 27 April 1994, up to the period of the next general election of 2 June 1999. The social, political and economic factors that have dominated this period have been of immense interest both nationally and internationally. The intrigue surrounding the inevitable switching of power from more than three hundred years of White political and economic domination to African majority rule was what caught the attention of the entire world (Sparks, 1994). A central concern here is the position of the minorities in this emerging transitional democracy. The world would not have been surprised if the country deteriorated into a state of civil war and if the most powerful of its minorities, the Whites, engaged in a protracted war to claim their own territory and self-rule. Indeed, such attempts were made by right-wingers, among Afrikaners and Zulus, but without much success. The periods of ethnic and racial tension were short lived and dissipated through careful maneuvering, especially through the leadership and charisma of the country's first African President, Nelson Mandela. Among the diversity of ethnic and racial groups, Afrikaners and Zulus considered themselves threatened minorities and articulated their fears in emotive rhetoric and acts of violence. While other minorities such as Indians and Coloureds reacted more passively to change. The options that were available to both these population groups restricted them to the type of actions that are expected of a minority, in Gellner's terms, an interest group. Such a group exists in relation to a more politically assertive majority referred to as a corporate group. The minority status and minimal integration of Indians into the military structures forbade them from responding to transformation in the ways that Afrikaners and Zulus had done. In addition, the growing negativity internationally and nationally towards political leadership under the African National Congress (ANC) raises a number of concerns about the future of democracy and the state. At issue is the increasing tendency of the state to ignore public outcries about corruption, mismanagement and incompetence at all levels of government and the civil service, as the transformation continues to unfold and consolidate itself in a climate of African empowerment. Given Africa's history of transition from colonial domination to majority rule and its impact on White and Indian minorities, this concern becomes even more pertinent to transformation in South Africa. A glimpse into how transformation impacted upon one of South Africa's minority population groups *viz.* people of Indian origin is provided below. In view of this selective approach, the following issues will assist in contextualising the study: justification for the study, contextualising class and ethnicity, the areas of fieldwork, methodology—literature survey and fieldwork.

The Issues: Justification for the Study

Not long after South Africa came under ANC domination in April 1994 allegations of mismanagement, incompetence in public office and a serious lack of transparency and accountability continued to appear in the media. At least two years before the end of Nelson Mandela's reign as President in the first five years of democracy, concerns were being raised about the competencies about his successor and his ability to create a climate of confidence in the future of the country. This did little to stem the tide of concern that was growing at a rapid pace. As the country surged towards a crisis in leadership and the quest for power revolved around individuals from the dominant African ethnic categories, other minorities such as Indians could only remain passive in these struggles. Although diverse in their geographical origins in India and in religion and languages, Indians as a minority had to choose the path of internal amnesia (Gellner, 1986) to claim the right to survival in South Africa (Singh, 1997). The ethnographic information in this project is a fitting tribute to Brass's (1985) description of what interest groups (ethnic minorities) have, as opposed to corporate rights (ethnic majority). Almost all of the interviewees articulated their concerns about post-apartheid South

Africa in terms of civil issues rather than political rights or aspirations of acquiring highest forms of political representation. They were more interested, as an interest group, in their economic and social well-being. Their important concern was the rapid decline in confidence on education, law and order, justice, affirmative action and their perceptions that they were being marginalised despite their historical disadvantages and involvement in the politics for a democratic South Africa. An anomaly in state policy on affirmative action which includes Coloureds and Indians as being previously disadvantaged and who therefore, should enjoy equal access to employment as Africans, but is perceived as being continuously ignored, has added to their feelings of insecurity. The effect of this has been more fear and anxiety than militant responses among most Indians, giving rise to the culturalisation of politics rather than the politicisation of culture (see Singh, 1997). This is different from the politics of 'proto-nations', to which Eriksen (1993: 124-5) refers, or the 'ethnicisation' that is taking place in contemporary world politics. Proto-nations is a reference to ethnic groups that mobilise support for secession and full independence, while ethnicisation is considered to be the equivalent of the politicisation of culture. Eriksen's position in the latter concept is too restrictive when compared with the politics of interest groups such as people of Indian origin in South Africa. Ethnicisation does not have to be confined to the politicisation of culture only, if it is to be understood in Mare's (1992) terms *i.e.* the tendency to adopt violent overtones. The concept is a much broader one and is capable of embracing more passive approaches to ethnic politics that are demonstrated by Brass's concept of interest groups.

In the late 1960s the Economic Commission for Latin America, dominated by the underdevelopment/dependency school and inspired by Andre Gunder Frank (1969), came to enjoy predominance in explaining the position of peripheral countries in the world political economy. This school emphasised the unequal relationship between the industrialised west and the developing countries that were the chief supplier of minerals and raw materials. While their analysis was initially centred on economic explanations, they soon realised the character of their political leadership, the low levels of skills, and the class and ethnic composition of the Latin American populace. This often gave way not just in Latin America but in Africa as well to ethnic conflicts, despotic and corrupt leadership, and even lesser commitment from the ruling elite to steer countries away from such quagmires. In South Africa as democracy unfolds and entrenches itself—a country with a comparatively impressive infrastructure and impressive economic outputs—it will become increasingly important to examine the perceptions that the newly elected government of the ANC has created up to June 1999.

In addressing South Africa's imminent transition to democracy and focussing on policy perspectives for the future, Schlemmer (1991: 15) argued that politics in South Africa is often oversimplified and has weakened the capacity of South African social science to deal with the real complexities of change in the system. Often, the competition for political power is seen as a Black (African)-White divide that ignores the role and contribution of other minorities such as Indians in regional and national politics. Schlemmer added that the models for transition in Southern Africa are distinctly unappetizing, especially when viewed against the background of the widespread problems in the sub-continent since independence. Post-independence leaders in Africa misled themselves into believing that they could administer their countries adequately without the assistance of their White adversaries. Half of White Rhodesians fled Zimbabwe—which was starving of foreign capital, Lesotho was under prolonged military rule, Mozambique and Angola were implementing scientific social re-education camps, and had crude East European equipment which could not be repaired. The consequences of all of these efforts were disastrous and had to be abandoned for lack of creative and responsible leadership. Other writers such as Good (1999) have supported this claim by illustrating how the rise of wealth and power within the cattle owning economy of Botswana has been accompanied by the creation of poverty and weakness. Olivier de Sardan (1999: 28) unhesitatingly placed the failures in Africa in the 'corruption complex', because as he puts it "Corruption (that is to say the 'corruption complex') has become, in almost all African countries, a common and routine element of the functioning of the administrative and para-administrative apparatus, from top to bottom."

South Africa too is showing similar signs in the rise of African elitism, decline in state capacity, embezzlement and predominance (as Good refers to the African leadership), is swiftly turning democracy into mere electoralism. Human, financial, organisational, and material resources have been dissipated on a very large scale. After the 1994 election, "the government, in the assessment of the Minister of Public Service and Administration, decided 'unscientifically' on a target of cutting 300,000 civil service jobs in three years, and wasted R1000 million on programmes which robbed the bureaucracy of its best brains, but retained those, whom Zola Skweyiya said, 'you would like to have retrenched' " (Good, 1997: 548). But recognition of Africa's leadership crisis did not go totally unrecognised. For instance, the late Mozambican President Samora Machel said to President Robert Mugabe soon after he took over Zimbabwe: *"Keep your Whites."* (Richburg, 1997: 191).

Despite the lessons of the continent's recent history of divided racial relationships, South Africa is going through another period of re-racialisation. While affirmative action and Black empowerment is selectively targeting Africans, it is simultaneously marginalizing previously disadvantaged groups such as Indians and Coloureds—despite them being part of the rubric of "Blacks" during the years of anti-apartheid struggle as well as being catered for in the policies pertaining to affirmative action. For this reason this book's focus is on race and ethnic relations in South Africa in the post-April 1994 period, with particular reference to the Indian minority. For more than four decades, since 1948, legislation required citizens to determine their aspirations along ethnic and racial lines. The 1950 Population Registration Act which divided South Africa's population into four racial categories *viz.* White, Indian, Coloured and African, and which also further divided Africans by ethnic group, provided the basis for differentiated access to economic and political opportunities. This gave rise to a significant degree of in-group solidarity within the racial and ethnic categories as each tried to either protect their privileges or oppose the constrictions that were imposed upon them. Out of this situation emerged cleavages that demand that the transformation process in post-Apartheid South Africa be as sensitive to racial and ethnic issues as possible. This situation exists at a time when ethnic tensions and acts of genocide in countries such as Rwanda, Burundi, Nigeria, Yugoslavia, Chechnya and Dagestan, among others, have produced more problems than solutions for peaceful coexistence in heterogeneous societies. The end of the Cold War has ushered in an unbridled build-up of arms in many of these strife torn countries and has spurred new kinds of political demands through mass ethnic mobilisation. Understanding Indians perceptions of and responses to transformation would, therefore, require some attention to the politics of such countries, but particularly that of Africa, since what happens in this continent has greater relevance than the problems that emerge from other continents.

A significant comment by a student was once made in seminar on the politics in Africa. In March 1997 when I took an M.A. class in Social Policy comprising mainly African students, a debate emerged around the topic of the role of the state and international aid in developing countries. This was the period during which Mobuto Sese-seko was facing firm opposition from the Laurent Kabila led forces in what was then Zaire—presently renamed the Democratic Republic of Congo. Most of the students were vociferously against the agendas of the international "donor" agencies. Enthusiasm among them to bash the International Monetary Fund and the World Bank for its role in Africa reached emotional levels, especially with reference to what little economic and political stability they brought to Zaire. Their accounts of how Sese-seko was co-opted and neutralised by these institutions and their surrogate multinational corporations, as they plundered the economic resources of the country, demonstrated a high level of political consciousness among the students. They evidently wanted to see a South Africa free from the alliances with such exploitative international agencies, trusting that the ANC led government was going to steer clear of them. But their enthusiasm was dampened and brought to an abrupt halt by an incisive response from a Nigerian student who retorted: *"Listen my South African brothers and sisters, the problem in Africa is not with the external powers. The problem here is that African leaders are weak and they have sold us out. Do you know if you have a referendum in Zaire today the people will ask for the French to return, and if you have a referendum in Nigeria today, they will ask for the British to return. That is because most of my country's oil revenue has been stolen by the Nigerian army generals who have put all the money in the Swiss banks—more than four hundred billion U.S. dollars! I am telling you, the Nigerian leaders have put my country five hundred years behind time.... If you look at the problem facing your own country today, it is going the same way with corruption. You will learn very soon...."*

In a sense, the student's statement enjoyed resonance with views that were generally associated with conservative thinking during apartheid, although he was certainly not influenced by it. His disappointment emerged out of his experiences in his own country, which had the misfortune of several *coup d'etats* in less than ten years. The political emancipation in most African countries after colonialism has been stifled by lack of vision, systematic plundering of state resources and mismanagement of the positive financial reserves and functional infrastructures that were left behind (Hyden, 1983; Hill, 1986; Good, 1986; Carmen, 1996). A classic case in point is provided in Hill's (1986) coverage of Kwame Nkrumah's People's Party's attempt to acquire support in the 1950s by providing cocoa farmers with official grants for replanting of their cocoa farms after they were devastated by swollen shoot disease. There was no account of how these funds were actually used and no threat of farms being expropriated if the grants were not repaid through increased production, until years later when a commission of inquiry discovered that farmers were putting the money to other uses. A widespread practice was to devote the cash to building houses in Accra for letting, leading to a sharp reduction in cocoa production and consequently to a reduction in state and foreign revenue. Similarly, Good's (1986) investigation into the massive annual losses of maize in Zambia in the 1980s, led him to discover a virtual absence of proper planning and massive pilfering of funds in almost every state Ministry. Every year there was insufficient fuel, no spare parts for transport vehicles, insufficient jute bags to store the maize, no grading of roads—making it difficult for trucks to collect the maize during the rainy season from farms away from the main road, no foreign currency to pay for overseas purchases, among a range of other problems. In Zimbabwe as well the central province of Gokwe continues to suffer isolation from the rest of the country because of the lack of proper infrastructure that should allow for dual movements of supplies in and out of the region (Breslin, 1994). While the farmers sell their produce to the neighbouring towns and cities there is no in-flow of goods to Gokwe that allows for ready access to basic goods and immediate needs. This has produced a desperate situation that has led people to eating dogs and adding grass to their maize meal in order to stretch its lasting capacity. Farmers have also been forced to sell their implements to buy food and pay for their children's education in order to break their reliance on agriculture. Such situations across Africa has led Hyden (1983: x), in his search for alternative forms of governance in the continent, to comment:

> As most of Africa's new states are reaching the age of a human generation, very few can look back on a period of real progress... To many foreign businesses eager to find new markets and new wealth, Africa has become a pit that swallows their money with little or no return. This is a judgement that applies not only to 'socialist' or 'Marxist-Leninist' regimes but also to those characterised by a 'free' economy, for example Nigeria, Sudan and Zaire... In spite of receiving colossal amounts of aid, they

> argue, countries like Tanzania and Zambia show no progress; instead their economies show signs of moving backwards....

Soon after the end of colonial rule Whites, who were the most privileged in the civil service and who were selectively trained to operate it, emigrated in droves to the industrialised countries. This migratory movement created a vacuum in administrative positions that made it difficult for the newly independent countries to effectively continue with the functioning of state structures in sustainable ways. Throughout sub-Saharan Africa the state has all but lost its role as the instrument for development and political stability. In other countries such as Rwanda, Burundi, Nigeria, Sudan and Somalia, the state has been instrumental in fostering political instability and the breakdown of civil society (Richburg, 1998) and of infrastructural developments. Interviewees for this project were aware of these situations and were generally critical of them. The expulsion of the Indians from Uganda in 1974, the restrictions imposed by the governments of Malawi and Tanzania on Indians to freely engage in commercial activities, and the carefully orchestrated ethnic clashes in KwaZulu-Natal in 1949 and 1985 between Africans and Indians were often points of reference in discussions on African domination. Since the beginning of 2000, President Robert Mugabe's threats to expropriate farmland owned by White farmers in Zimbabwe, and in April 2001 his inaction against foreign interests by self-styled war veterans, have added to this list of references in conversations on African majority rule.

These failures in the African countries had been put to significant use by successive apartheid regimes in South Africa since 1948—when mobilisation for decolonisation in Africa started increasing at a rapid pace. But the move towards the creation of nation-states in Africa has led to more problems than solutions (Davidson, 1992; Bayart, 1993). Davidson (pp. 99-101) for instance has argued that nation-statism was only a form of escapism from colonial domination. In their attempts to transform colonial territories into national territories, Africans found their wealth of ethnic cultures distracting, hard to absorb and retrogressive—especially in its violent manifestations. By drawing attention to these situations, Apartheid's propogandists succeeded in persuading large segments of the Indian and Coloured populations, and to a smaller extent the African population, of the dangers of African majority rule. The consequences of these campaigns over the four decades of apartheid rule was that more than sixty per cent of the

Indian voting population voted for the National Party in the April 1994 general election while a bigger number among the Coloureds in the Western Cape did the same for the National Party, making them the regional government for the Western Cape.

It is against this background of perceptions of disorderliness in Africa and the emerging democracy in South Africa that the topic has been conceptualised. Perceptions are important in formulating responses to change, especially in a situation where the political and economic conditions are volatile and prone to negative national and international reactions, as has been the case in South Africa since the mid-1980s.

The end of apartheid has brought the issues of restructuring and transformation in South Africa into sharp prominence. Drastic changes had to be effected to ensure that the newly elected government, dominated by the African National Congress (ANC), maintained its support base within the African population and within segments of the Coloured, Indian, and to a lesser extent White populations. The dissolution of the ten 'tribally' based homelands that had a semblance of self-governance imposed upon them during apartheid, as well as the range of prohibitive race based laws that applied to all of South Africa, had resulted in a unified state where race and ethnicity were bound to be radically reviewed. After centuries of systematic exclusion of those who were not previously classified as "White", from the mainstreams of political and economic life, these arenas had suddenly witnessed an influx of Africans, Coloureds and Indians. The rights of these previously disenfranchised racial categories, particularly the African majority, have become the cornerstone of transformation policies. It has raised acute questions about how to deliver social services to what is seen as a differentiated motley of people spread across the length and breadth of South Africa. Although the tendency was to refer to all previously disenfranchised citizens as "Black", the situation is no longer considered with the same zeal. Indians in KwaZulu-Natal and Coloureds in the Western Cape are deemed to have enjoyed more privileges than Africans. This has created a schism in the rank and file of these population groups and has retained the notions of race, class and ethnicity with the same zeal that they had during Apartheid.

Contextualising Class and Ethnicity

Understanding the perceptions of and responses to transformation among people of Indian origin has to be examined in the context of the debates around race, class, ethnicity and civil society in South Africa. These aspects are unlikely to disappear in the foreseeable future and will in all likelihood continue to determine the nature and pace of transformation. A sociologist-*cum*-cynic and critic of South Africa's transformation, Desai (1999: 81), stated in a comment on the swift rise of the new African elite and the flight of capital to overseas stock exchanges: "Those who are not part of the political class or who are not wealthy do not have the luxury of temporary sojourns in foreign lands. For the middle class who wish to test the waters overseas, the only option is to accumulate capital by selling up to finance their trip. The lower classes, of course, cannot even emigrate to the next province."

Pluralists have written critically on the nature of race and class relations in South Africa. A prolific writer from this tradition, van den Berghe (1969), argued that social classes in the Marxian sense of the relationships to the means of production exist by means of definition, as they must in any capitalist country, but they are not meaningful social realities. Clearly, pigmentation, rather than ownership of land or capital is the most significant criterion of status in South Africa. Wolpe (1988) challenged this position by arguing that van den Berghe makes class irrelevant and socio-economic differences are treated as the outcome of racial definitions. The relationships between social groups are viewed as a function of racial ideology, attitudes and prejudices. To Wolpe (1988), the net result of not accounting for race prejudice in structural terms means that the bulk of the writing on race in South Africa, remains at a descriptive level only.

More recent analyses have gone beyond such limitations by examining the dynamics of power politics and the emergent political partnerships that are based more on the interests of capital rather than on race alone. Both issues however are inseparable from each other. To Glaser (1997: 23) there are several trends that are shaping relations between the (ANC-governed) state and 'black' civil society in the country. These trends emerge out of a commitment to reduce White political and economic hegemony and engage in the process of African empowerment. But they are also constrained by the interests of capital and the reality of an untrained African labour force and white-collar personnel which is presently incapable of assuming total responsibility of the country's administration. However, Glaser's reference to 'black' civil society is not an inclusive reference to all the previously disadvantaged groups, in that it is restricted to Africans only and ignores Coloureds and Indians.

Macdonald's (1996) paper on Power Politics in South Africa amplifies the trends identified by Glaser in two ways. First, he sees the state being exposed to relentless pressure to adopt policies preferred by capital, which exerts a steady conservative influence on the ANC, and second he feels that the terms negotiated in the interim constitution specifically protect the integrity of established bureaucracies. These factors have a stifling effect on the ANC's welfare policies over the African working classes, forcing the party to reorient itself by shifting its political base from popular organisations to state bureaucracies. It is in this maneuver that the contradictions and preoccupation with race and ethnicity in post-Apartheid transformation is raised. Filatova's (1997) commentary on the ANC's discussion document on *Nation-Formation and Nation Building* is an apt illustration of how South Africa is being re-racialised through pronounced efforts towards an Africanist state. She warns that another new development is that Africanism as a perception (not a distinct political movement or party) has gained momentum more than ever before both inside and outside the ranks of the ANC and its allies. Filatova (1997: 52) succinctly captures the current mood in the transformation process by stating: "The reassertion of African pride, the invention and the re-invention of black identity, styles and fashions, culture, even ideology (*ubuntu)* the discovery of 'Africaness', even if only in the form of renaming of places and personalities, the re-invention and revision of a black legacy in search of a new, particularly African way—all this is a natural reaction to the past." As one of the most stable and developed countries in the continent, South Africa is presently trying to position itself as a major role player and moral leader in Africa. "The first step to achieve this is 'Africanisation' of the image of the country in both cultural and ideological sense. The nervous reaction of the government to the signs of rejection by other African states of South Africa's leading role on the continent on the grounds that it is not African enough (Nigeria's challenge to Mandela being one such example) betrayed a lack of confidence of its own position in this matter" (Filatova, 1997: 53). Therefore, in the context of re-engineering civil society in South Africa as well as the country's position on the African continent, the challenge lies with how the ANC can establish and sustain an acceptable level of Africanism and make it coexist through racial and ethnic harmony. Despite the party's emphasis on non-racialism before the 1994 election, the vote was racially divided and it emerged overwhelmingly 'African'. As a result of this political emotions and feelings of the 'non-African' minorities play a much smaller role in the ANC's political considerations now than they had before the 1994 election.

At a national level there is much talk about the African Renaissance in the entire continent—a concept that is still short of a proper definition and seriously lacking in direction. Coined and nurtured by Thabo Mbeki, the rhetoric on the issue and the realities by which South Africa and the rest of Africa is presently confronted, raise a number of questions about what he hopes to achieve. While his recognition, that violent conflict in the continent is the most inhibiting factor, does carry weight, it ignores the seriousness and equally damaging effects of embezzlement of public funds, lack of transparency and accountability by politicians and the growing tendency towards authoritarianism. Propaganda on the Renaissance ignores two fundamental issues *i.e.* the absence of sufficient numbers of adequately trained Africans to assume management of the country's economy and politics, as well as the problems of race and ethnicity. The ethnic/racial cleavages that South Africans still have to confront in order to create a situation, as Huntington (1968: 4-5) stated, to bring about political stability through an approach that will converge equality of political participation with the art of living together. But contemporary conditions can hardly provision such a scenario as the euphoria and optimism of the pre- and post-1994 election periods continues to wear out. This situation has trapped the intellectuals, in Sitas's (1998: 37) terms, "between utopian and dystopian forms of thinking." To Sitas, dystopian thinking has both an analytical and a moral core that on the one hand magnifies social trends and tendencies and, on the other, warns of anti-social outcomes. By contrast, utopian thinking wilfully ignores such trends by keeping people in a false state of optimism. This comparison is a result of Sitas's (1995) earlier ominous warnings about the serious threats to the democratic and socialist vision of the liberation movement in South Africa and a marked disintegration of the movement itself. This is already evident in the unveiling of evidence in an arms scandal in 2000 that implicates senior ANC officials in a manner that has done irreparable damage to the movement, and in the April 2001 saga, played out publicly, of an alleged plot by senior members of the ANC to unseat President Thabo Mbeki.

The roots of these problems are deeply entrenched in the difficulties, the ANC is facing with its redistributive policies, in African empowerment and the incredibly endemic levels of mismanagement.

These unavoidable promises, which the ANC rightfully had to make, inevitably reintroduces the dynamics of racial and ethnic discourses, as much as the ANC may wish to publicly, but unrealistically and untruthfully, pursue a line of non-racialism. The ANC could benefit significantly by taking a leaf out of Horowitz's book (1991: 85) in which he has realistically stressed the need to recognise the importance of racial, ethnic and sub-ethnic identities in South Africa. He has warned that some inter-group cleavages have considerable conflict-producing potential, as witnessed in the rest of post-Independence Africa's conflict and violence. He is pointedly crude about the fact that it is a fallacy of the 1950s and 1960s that an inclusive nationalism would be the universal solvent of differences. In fact, South Africa's constitution, often hailed as one of the best in the world, is actually outdated by virtue of its emphasis on human and individual rights (Singh, 1999). We are now living in an era that is paying increasing attention to multi-culturalism and minority rights in order to minimise militancy and fragmentation of the populations. Recent trends have shown, as Filatova's (1997) paper also testifies, that South Africa's politics will not be non-racial and non-ethnic, but multi-racial and multi-ethnic. Horowitz rightfully cautions us that "Once the democratic process cracks under the strain of ethnic conflict and of parties aligned with particular ethnic groups—whether the crack comes from a military coup or the inauguration of a single party state—the way is open for much smaller minorities to rule behind the façade of an allegedly inclusive single party. That possibility cannot be excluded for South Africa unless powerful precautions are taken" (Horowitz, 1991: 86). At present, the ANC has not produced any clarification, in their document on *Nation-Formation and Nation Building,* between expressions such as "the affirmation of our Africanness as a nation" and "equality among the racial, ethnic, language, cultural and religious communities' within 'a united nation', 'multiple identities' in the melting pot of broad South Africanism" (Filatova, 1997: 55).

These developments must also be viewed against two issues *viz.* increasing ethnic differentiation and the rising ethnic tensions in the 1990s throughout the world, where the result has been large-scale acts of genocide and ethnic cleansing. In countries such as Rwanda, Nigeria, and Yugoslavia the high levels of ethnocentrism has translated into the most violent forms of ethnic warfare that was widely expected to occur in South Africa after the demise of White rule. In such multi-cultural societies majority segments of the populations have used the democratic processes to dominate in political and economic spheres. There has been a strong tendency to consolidate the state by appealing to the nationalism of the majority people (Miall, 1994). As a result of this, ethnic minorities in different countries in several parts of the world have experienced varying forms of isolation, intimidation and violence against them. Referring to the Minority Rights Group, Miall (1990: xiv) presents their definition of an ethnic minority as: "…a group which is numerically inferior to the rest of the population in a society, which is politically non-dominant and which is being reproduced as an ethnic category." For a minority to exist, there has to be a majority and *vice-versa.* During the apartheid era in South Africa, race and ethnicity were fundamental in determining political, economic and social boundaries, enforced through legislation. In post-apartheid South Africa these boundaries are supposed to dissipate through a non-racial ideology. A fundamental question—for which there is no simple explanation—is: "Can the boundaries created by race and class during apartheid, be transcended by the creation of a new African elite, by acting dismissively towards Indians and Coloureds in affirmative action, and by the rise in Africanist tendencies in government, to bring about a new and more patriotic South African identity?"

This question must be examined against the experiences of other such groups in multi-cultural societies in other parts of the world. The violent experiences of ethnic minorities have often militantly raised the issues of rights and obligations of minorities. The rights of minorities to receive equal treatment, practice their religion and normative customs, and to speak, learn and teach their languages have become prerequisites for their full participation in the political and economic life of the state. Their obligations and patriotism to the state are determined by the measures in which these requirements are met. Failure of the state to meet them either in part or adequately can result, as experience has demonstrated, in violent action for secession or independence. The salience of the minority problem throughout the world has produced a transnational regime for minority rights (Miall, 1994: 3). But it is still relatively weak and centred mainly around the concerns of minorities in Europe. It offers protection under international law and international conventions such as the European Convention on Political Rights, and requires subscription to the political commitments that have been determined by member-states of the Conference on Security and Cooperation in Europe (CSCE). However weak such a forum might be, it is a start. Its existence is indicative of the requirements of states throughout the world to seriously consider the needs of its minorities in order to ensure that they carry out their obligations with the enthusiasm that is required of loyal citizens.

In South Africa, people of Indian origin have especially one thing in common *i.e.* their ancestral geographical roots in India. Otherwise there is a diversity of groups among them who differ from one another through language, religion, regional roots, economic status, eating habits and taboos, personal preferences, and above all, class differences. Ginwala (1974) points out that until the end of indenture, divisions among Indians along lines of language, culture, religion and juridical status, coincided with economic divisions. The indentured Indians were largely Tamil-Telugu, South Indian Hindus, while the unencumbered immigrants who followed them were mainly Gujarati Muslims from Western India. Although the Indians were responding to restrictions formulated in racial terms, Ginwala found that they did not respond as an ethnic unit. The particular interests of the different segments determined the nature of their political participation. This view was supported by Vahed (1995) who acknowledged that Indians formed their own social and economic pyramid. He argued that merchants had a choice to identify with the White bourgeoisie or disregard their conveniences in favour of identification with the wider struggle for political emancipation. The Indian middle class only had the privileges of protected employment, but like their counterparts in the working class, they were equally constrained and precluded from being absorbed into the wider society.

Such diversity among Indians in South Africa diminishes any notion that assumes homogeneity within this commonly referred group. Despite these wide-ranging differences among the various segments, there is still the tendency to refer to people of Indian origin as "Indians" in various contexts and discourses. In this sense, the simplistic and uncritical definition of ethnicity that is provided by Eriksen (1993: 6) is useful. The term ethnicity refers to relationships between groups whose members within each group consider themselves to be distinctive, and these groups may be ranked hierarchically within a society. However, the problem with this definition is that it imputes a notion of homogeneity in social and economic status of very large segments in a country's population. It does not focus on social stratification within ethnic categories and precludes understanding of how economic status and linkages can cut across social boundaries that produce situational conditions that may for instance temporarily ignore ethnic distinctions. In this context, the concept is useful to Indians as an ethnic category only in so far as it refers to people of a common geographical origin, and not for any other descriptive purpose. For this reason the economic segments that exist within the Indian population also require a class analysis of historical and contemporary experiences, revolving around perceptions of and responses to transformation. This is based on the assumption that people from different socio-economic backgrounds are likely to perceive transformation and respond to it in terms of their levels of education, awareness and political consciousness, personal experiences and resources at their disposal. Restriction to any particular economic segment of the Indian population would have produced a limited perspective of how Indians are responding to the radical political changes since April 1994. While there might be perceptions that transcend class boundaries among Indians, the responses can only be determined by their skills and resource bases.

The interviewees for this study had earning capacities and material conditions that were evidently different and it was assumed that their responses would vary accordingly. People of different class backgrounds have achieved varying levels of education, which in turn determines their levels of consciousness and responses to the political and economic conditions in the country. For instance, there have been regular media reports of people wanting to emigrate to the industrialised countries, with lawyers and other recruiting agents advertising extensively to exploit this market. The countries that are being extensively advertised are England, United States of America, Canada, Australia and New Zealand. Emigration is only one of the factors that has become a major phenomenon in post-apartheid South Africa. Other phenomena that have acquired equally serious public attention include:

- unbridled proliferation of squatters in urban areas,
- violent crime,
- widespread allegations of official embezzlement of state funds, and
- lack of vision by the state to produce effective policies in key areas such as health, education, and law and order.

Race has been an important factor in linking especially the latter issues to specific classified groups. During apartheid, it was Whites who were held responsible, and since April 1994 the association has been with Africans. It would be naive to deny that squatters and violent crime are not especially associated with Africans in South Africa, although every other population category has its share of the same. There is almost a tacit acknowledgement of these perceptions in the media and with different racial and ethnic groups, especially when the virtually hopeless conditions in other parts of Africa are compared with what is occurring in post-apartheid South Africa. It is against the background of these dominant factors that the perceptions of and responses to transformation among people of Indian origin were approached.

The Areas of Fieldwork

Research was carried out in several suburbs in the Greater Durban Region that extends to Stanger on the north coast and to Umzinto on the south coast. The core areas of research were Phoenix, Reservoir Hills, Clare Estate, Overport, Asherville, Verulam and Tongaat. Other areas where research was done on a smaller scale were Umkoomaas, Umzinto and Stanger. These are 'marginal' farming areas which were followed up through networking with interviewees from the core areas of research. The suburbs were deliberately chosen because they constituted a mixture of people from working/underclass, middle class and upper class backgrounds. Phoenix is the area with mainly working class/under class people who rented in municipal housing, while the other areas had mainly middle class civil servants, self-employed professionals and a sprinkling of big farmers and industrialists who lived in a variety of self-owned houses. In several of the middle class suburbs working class people who rented in houses were also interviewed.

All of the areas were classified during the apartheid era as Indian Group Areas under the Group Areas Act of 1950. They were, therefore, still predominantly occupied by people of Indian origin. Purchase and sale of property in these areas were previously restricted to Indians only. But since the repeal of the Influx Control Laws that used to forbid Africans from becoming permanent citizens in South Africa's metropolitan areas, the demographics in these suburbs have changed drastically. The rapid migration of Africans from the rural areas and violence ridden urban townships have led to an influx of people into the urban areas, where they started building squatter camps. This gave rise to significant changes to the dynamics of the quiet and relatively 'undisturbed' suburban lifestyle of the Indian population. It is the changes in these suburbs that have made them attractive for the topic at hand. Their significance lies in examining the impact of these and the broader political changes that are perceived to be taking place after years of legally imposed racial boundaries and insulated lifestyle that was effected through the 1950 Group Areas Act.

Methodology: Literature Survey and Fieldwork

Literature Survey

The first attempt at understanding Indians in South Africa began with an exercise to understand the dynamics of poverty in the Indian township of Phoenix. This was followed by an historical literature survey and analysis of two violent clashes between the regionally dominant African population *viz.* the Zulus and Indians in 1949 and 1985 respectively (see Singh, 1992). The literature on these two episodes provided a glimpse into information that raised more questions than provided solutions for my initial efforts on understanding the nature of the clashes between the two groups. It brought into focus a complex range of issues that required more than a cursory examination of the ethnic tensions between two of the major ethnic groups in KwaZulu-Natal. Among these issues were the history of colonialism and Indian indentured labour, the dynamics of Indo-European relations, the dynamics of caste and class among Indians, their participation in politics at regional and national levels, their responses to change in the face of the collapse of apartheid, and the future of civil society in post-apartheid South Africa.

The experiences of Indians during colonialism up to 1910, after the formation of the Union Government in 1910, during Apartheid since 1948, and up to 1961 when they were granted permanent citizenship for the first time, provide relevant insights into the ethnically and racially divisive way in which South Africa was administered. Literature that covered these periods, produced mainly by historians, broadly covered a range of issues that highlighted the blatant racism that Indians had to face on a daily basis (Sannyasi and Benarsidas, 1931; Joshi, 1942; Calpin, 1949; Pachai, 1979; Bhana and Brain, 1990; *among a range of others*). These references dealt extensively and intensively on legislation that was specifically designed to restrict Indians from free and equal participation in the country's economy. On the contrary, anthropological and sociological research paid little or no attention to the hardships that Indians had faced, or how the constrictive legislative devices manifested to constrain Indian advancement. While the sociologist Meer (1969) acknowledges these issues, she treated them in a dismissive manner, focussing more on the achievements of a small segment of Indians and generalising upon them rather than on the shoddy experiences of the majority. Anthropologists such as Kuper (1956, 1957, 1960) and Jithoo (1978; 1985), who have been the main contributors to ethnographic studies on Indians, produced descriptive functionalist accounts of Hindu social structures and Indian business families respectively. More critical insights into the nature and dynamics of people of Indian origin came from Ginwala (1974) and Vahed (1995) on issues of class consciousness and control, and the making of an Indian identity respectively. A related Masters dissertation by sociologist Maharaj (1995) on the social identities of Indians in a changing South Africa had some relevance as well. But her information was mainly statistical and highly generalised without proper reference to class or caste based responses to change and identity. Only one chapter out of seven dealt with empirical data that was limited to commentary on responses that were tabulated rather than on analysis and interpretation.

Despite South Africa's comparatively favourable economic position with the rest of its African counterparts, it was the racism, unrepresentative political structures, and mismanagement of the economy that eventually led to the demise of the apartheid state. Political structures and economic opportunities were best developed for Whites and to a lesser extent for the other population groups. Huntington (1968: 3), in describing the increasing gap between the rich and poorer nations, aptly pointed out that in the twentieth century, the principal locus of political underdevelopment, like economic underdevelopment, tends to be the modernising countries of Asia, Africa and Latin America. Apart from a few exceptions, the political evolution of these countries after the Second World War was characterised by increasing ethnic and class conflict, recurring rioting and mob violence, frequent military *coups d'etat,* the dominance of unstable personalistic leaders who often pursued disastrous economic and social policies, widespread and blatant corruption among cabinet ministers and civil servants, and declining standards of bureaucratic efficiency and performance. Ironically, press reports and other areas of the media abound with such information on the performance of the ANC, since its inception as the government. The Heath Commission, especially appointed to expose rogue elements in the civil service, has revealed massive corruption in almost every ministry, regionally and nationally. By July 1999 the auditor-general's report stated that the recoveries, savings and prevention of loss by the Commission was at least R1.38 billion (rands). This included the prevention of a loss of property worth R385 million (rands), where state assets had not been transferred but were in the process of being embezzled or lost due to maladministration (*Daily News,* 22 July 1999). The South African Television (SATV) network's *am2day* (6 October 1999) reported that the Commission had an astronomical figure of 220,000 cases on their list. South Africa's battle against inefficiency and embezzlement of state funds was compounded by the lack of ingredients that has put other Indo-Pacific Rim countries ahead of it in productive capacity for the new millennium. Sitas (1998: 38) and Macdonald (1996: 223) argue in slightly different ways about the negative impact of the country's scarcity of capital, its reliance on the International Monetary Fund and World Bank and the absence of a flexible and committed labour force to enhance capacity. These factors inhibit the redistributive commitments of the ANC, enhances the role of business and maintains much of the state organisation that was built up by the National Party during Apartheid. The impact of this has been an almost dubious retreat from the populist policies of the ANC and a new alliance with capital, which prompted Nelson Mandela to declare: "the ANC is in office, not in power" (*Cape Times*, 16 February 1995). The route towards acquiring power would be, as Filatova's (1997) paper implies, through Africanisation of state apparatuses and African domination in the centres of production and service delivery.

The only positive aspect in the literature about South Africa's transformation since 1994 is the relative coexistence of the different racial groups—achieved largely through the efforts of one senior statesman—ex-President Nelson Mandela. Otherwise it is an on-going saga of incapacitated state apparatuses and leadership at every level of the civil service.

Fieldwork

An undisturbed effort in fieldwork began in 1995 with a departmental project on squatters that afforded me the opportunity to investigate Indian residents responses to this phenomenon in the midst of their suburbs. Thereafter an opportunity for more research was presented in 1997 when the Centre for Science Development encouraged application for funding which required academics to build research capacity among disadvantaged students, particularly those of African background. One of the topics was on ethnic identity and social transformation in post-apartheid South Africa. This provided an ideal opportunity to use African post-graduate students to test two kinds of responses. The first was to test whether African students would have problems in interviewing Indians, while the second was to analyse responses from Indians on issues that were pertinent to the breakdown of apartheid and the voting in, for the first time in the country's history, of an African dominated government. Two Honours students, both Africans, were initially selected for this research capacity building exercise. One did thirty interviews with business people in the Point area of Durban's Central business district, while the second student did thirty interviews with residents in Phoenix. The students, a male and female, were generally well received by their interviewees and they found the experience, which was their first, rewarding. Thirty more interviews were done by three Indian students, as part of the research capacity building exercise in Sea Cow Lake, Newlands and Isipingo. A comparison in the experience between the Indian and African students showed no difference in receptivity by the interviewees. A letter of introduction from me helped in acquiring for them, in most instances, a sympathetic reception from most people who were approached. For the African students, racial intolerance was surprisingly not encountered at all. This was an important learning exercise for both the students and me in several ways, as outlined below.

Apart from the ninety interviews that was done by the students, an additional one hundred and sixty-five was carried out by myself. Eighty were done in the working class townships and eighty-five were done in the middle-class suburbs—including twenty form the outlying areas of Umzinto and Stanger. Both sets of areas were charcterised by a diversity that dispels the notion of homogeneity in living standards, resource availability, levels of education and levels of articulation and consciousness about political transformation. For instance, in the working class areas there were significant differences between the levels of education that people had and the resources that they had within the households. Many households had worked themselves up to positions of convenience that matched that of their middle-class counterparts and were very articulate on the post-1994 elections in South Africa. On the contrary, many middle-class residents had impressive collections of modern conveniences, but were woefully ignorant of the changes taking place around them. Their relative successes in their professions or businesses created a barrier between their material comforts and political consciousness.

The interviewing took place in varying contexts, such as in individual and group interviews, structured and semi-structured interviews—in homes, outside homes, in places of work and in social gatherings. Interviewing was often facilitated by regular periods of participant observation in various settings such as informal and formal social gatherings such as prayer rituals, weddings, funerals, public meetings, parties and sports fields, where large number of people were present. Each situation that was targeted for research required the adoption of criteria that was determined by the nature of the day's events and the kind of people who were present. In most instances, careful and calculated approaches to individuals and groups of individuals produced the information that was appropriate for the day. It also led to effective networking and following up on leads for future interviews. There are precedents in fieldwork that were set by the need to continuously adapt and improvise, as Burgess noted (1984: 5):

> The field researcher is a methodological pragmatist...The researcher is, therefore, engaged in a variety of tasks. A central feature of this work involves monitoring the research process and the research design. For the design will be continually modified and developed by the researcher throughout the project. Alongside observational work, formal and informal interviews may be conducted and life histories and personal documents may be collected.

In most personal and group interviews the life histories of individuals were central to ascertaining how their experiences determined their perceptions of and responses to transformation in post-apartheid South Africa. Participant observation, follow-up interviews and either deliberately or unintentionally meeting interviewees more than once, helped in establishing consistencies and inconsistencies in people's perceptions and responses to changes in the country. The participant observation approach was made possible in most cases through casual integration into the formal and informal gatherings and participating, in Blumer's (1966) words, in the position of an actor. Such an approach is qualitatively different from the objective approach in which the researcher stands as an outsider who assesses what he/she observes in terms of his/her understanding of events in a detached manner. For Blumer the most effective way to understand how 'actors' perceive situations is to become an actor on equal terms (see Burgess 1984: 4). Such an approach, however, is convenient for people who approach their research as 'insiders', in the sense that they belong to the same ethnic or interest group. Integration and acceptance into target groups is made easier through familiarity, identity and in a sense, undeclared solidarity. This enables researchers to become privy to the most intimate thoughts and discussions on ethnicity, change and how people embrace or reject it. Very often, even when researchers enter into situations that are not intended as ethnographic exercises, they have the advantage to complementing their data in the most unexpected ways and times. Such instances provide the 'insider' researcher with information that is unlikely to be gathered by those who approach their research as 'objective outsiders'. This is especially the case when people engage in discussion on issues that are sensitive, and ethnically and racially biased. Outsiders, especially if they belong to different ethnic or racial groups, are unlikely to become privy to uninhibited discussions with individuals who have a common social background. It is common human tendency for people to speak guardedly when they suspect that someone from outside their group is unlikely to take too kindly to their views and attitudes. This happens especially if that person/s either belongs to the opposition group under discussion or if what is spoken is likely to be challenged. Keesing (1981: 490) is, therefore, correct in stating that:

> "...there is some power in an insider's view as well: institutions can be brought to bear, and native actors can often see the oversimplifications and distortions of anthropology fieldwork—the costs of an 'outsider view'—are becoming painfully clear as students in formerly colonial areas learn what anthropologists have written about their people."

It is for these reasons that conversational analysis became an important mechanism for eliciting information in the research process. It helped to make sense of the discourses in formal and informal gatherings, the perceptions that were ascertained through speech from them, the responses in areas such as security measures that were outwardly visible and that recurred, and the interaction among those who were observed and/or interviewed. Conversational analysis is significant in understanding the nature of social structure in real life (Allen and Guy, 1978: 34). It is important in understanding how and where people place themselves in the social taxonomy of the multicultural nation-state in which they are a part. Verbal discourses and social interaction provide ample information on how people's aspirations are conditioned and dictated by existing economic and political realities. Inevitably, this determines the nature and extent of their acceptance or rejection of change and their levels of social interaction.

Among South Africa's racial and ethnic categories, the insulation that was imposed upon designated population groups during apartheid created mind-sets that produced social boundaries that constrained people to think along myopic lines. These factors present an important challenge for investigation in post-apartheid South Africa. This is why the perceptions of and responses to transformation among the country's minorities are important.

CHAPTER TWO

Perceptions from the Ground: From Euphoria to Despondency

Introduction

The first democratically held post-apartheid general election that was held in South Africa on April 27, 1994 generated a euphoria and excitement that reverberated positively throughout the length and breadth of the country. This occurred despite the assertion of Zulu and Afrikaner nationalism and the disruptions it generated. The African National Congress (ANC), which was the political party that was widely expected to win the general election, was generally successful in its campaign in creating a strong measure of confidence in the population by convincing the electorate on their ability to take over as the incumbent government.

The South African media, once notorious for its constant reference of the ANC as a terrorist organisation, had changed its discourse with more favourable reference to it. Its roie during apartheid was a distinctly biased position that favoured White minority rule. There were visible signs that the media had accepted the reality of political transformation and the unbanning of the African dominated political movements. Special supplements on voter education were periodically issued in all of the daily and weekend newspapers. In attempts to encourage voters' participation, it published responses from the public and encouraged them to participate in the election. While non-racialism and democracy were the cornerstones of the election, participation and assessment of the outcomes in racial terms was unavoidable. In one supplement of a daily newspaper a voter's viewpoint was recorded in the following words:

> "I'm so excited I can't even wait. People must learn to be more optimistic and patient. This is politics and cannot be solved overnight. I may be seen as Indian and better off, but I also never

had a chance to decide on this country's future. For the first time I'm going to decide on my future myself."

The media certainly helped in creating the required climate for free and fair elections—and it did take place in most parts of the country. Soon after the election the ANC was depicted as the only possible party to have been worthy of winning the election. For instance, the *Daily News* (3 May 1994) produced an article with a striking caption "*ANC'S election win a victory for the people*". The President elect, Nelson Mandela, declared himself ready to work with the leaders of the other political parties and appealed to South Africans to work together to heal old wounds. Many believed and correctly so that he was committed to this task. Such gestures brought many to present Mandela to the rest of the world with the status of a *messiah* and many began to see him in this light. Mandela epitomised the miracle that the world was looking for in South Africa—a person serious about and committed to non-violence—which could galvanise the diverse political forces and bring them to merge into a single political process, despite their differing ideologies. His international status and winning smile helped him to succeed admirably in this task.

The world as well as South Africans were pleasantly surprised to witness the first non-racial general election taking place with a minimum level of violence. The occasion was marked by long queues of people that stretched in many places for more than a kilometre. Voters from all the historically designated racial groups (Whites, Indians, Coloureds and Africans) stood together for hours before they got their opportunities to vote. It was generally a widespread and visibly light-hearted and jovial atmosphere. The Indian dominated residential areas that were under intense observation were Clare Estate, Reservoir Hills, Asherville and Overport. Besides Overport, which has a substantial Coloured population and which added to the racial diversity of the queues, the former three areas were predominantly Indian and to a lesser extent, African. However, despite the fact that these areas were designated Indian Group Areas during apartheid, and somewhat remain this way as a spill over from the apartheid era, many polling stations had queues that were predominantly African for large parts of the day. The reason for this was the unbridled proliferation of informal settlements in these areas. At this particular juncture there did not appear to be widespread concern or opposition to this situation. The positive outlook that the democratic elections engendered, especially through the ANC's promise to build one million houses in five years, subdued any major opposition from the residents, to Africans setting up shacks in close proximity to their houses. The need to accept and appreciate one another across the racial divide and to build a common future together acquired prominence over the more destructive elements that were unwilling to accept the changes that were taking place.

In some parts of the country the level of disruptions and violence did mar this otherwise acceptable and peaceful process. The internecine violence that occurred in these areas was deemed as the work of "third force" elements, in which the previous white dominated government of the National Party and the regionally based Inkhata Feedom Party in KwaZulu-Natal (Zulu dominated) was widely accused of being instrumental. In some areas voting was not possible because of the extent of interference by locally dominant politicians and their supporters who did not expect to win the election in their areas, while in other areas losers were expected to squeal over the results. On May 4, 1994, the *Daily News* produced an article with the caption: "*Massive election fraud*"—covering the accusations and counter accusations of electoral fraud by opposing politicians.

In an emulation of North American politics the ANC led government called for an assessment of their first one hundred days in office. After publicly calling for assessments Mandela stated that he felt positive about the Government of National Unity[1] and the country's relative calm. But criticism still abounded about there being no sign of how the Reconstruction and Development Programme was to be funded. In KwaZulu-Natal there was still no sign of collaboration between the IFP and ANC to end the violence and build the organs of democracy. Several months later, with the persistence of such problems, the *Daily News* (1 October 1994) editorial made the following comment:

> While much fault for the breakdown lies with the IEC, certain political leaders too must take the blame for needlessly exacerbating those doubts through rhetoric laced accusations of vote rigging by their opponents. It was crystally clear from the moment the count started that they were positioning themselves to repudiate the various outcomes and erode the legitimacy of the dominant party in the new legislature, if they fared poorly. Political parties have nonetheless declared themselves ready to endorse the elections as substantially free and fair."

Up until the middle of 1995 the socio-political ethos was characterised by widespread optimism and the recognition by most South Africans of the need to work together. There was renewed foreign investor confidence as well as local business sector enthusiasm. However, time had shown that this period was akin to riding on a crest—with the country's confidence levels on all fronts taking a nose-dive through rapid escalation of criminal violence[2] and organised crime.

After the Elections

The areas in which research was done showed visible signs of a population under siege. As crime spread to most parts of the country the populace started becoming more conscious of their personal and family safety and began taking measures to meet the challenges that it presented. Apartheid's segregation of the classified racial groups helped to maintain control of the disadvantaged masses, especially Africans, from the neighbouring townships and rural areas. It insulated them from the poverty, hunger and crime that became a characteristic of indigent African areas. But after the April 1994 general election this insulation was hampered even more by the proliferation of informal settlements in the empty spaces that permitted this phenomenon. Although the movement into traditionally "non-African" residential areas by Africans started prior to this period, in mid-1980s, when the influx control laws were relaxed and later repealed. For the first time middle class Indians were being exposed to the degree of deprivation, unemployment and crime that was already a part of the lifestyle of African townships almost since their inception. The gun licences by the Indian residents increased drastically. The number of licences that were awarded annually since 1994 was 431, for 1994 at least 577, for 1996 there were 420 (1997 not available) and 380 for 1998[3]. The reason for the downward turn in 1998 could only be based on conjecturing—that the state was determined to reduce the number of guns owned by citizens. In a random survey in February-March 1997, of 100 houses in three of the research areas *viz*. Reservoir Hills, Clare Estate and Asherville, sixty seven claimed to be either in possession of firearms, or in the process of acquiring them or were able to acquire them at short notice. Several of the respondents walked either with their guns around their hips in a somewhat openly provocative manner, or had them tied around their ankles in a holster. Of those who already had guns, eighteen made at least one of four claims, that they had been forced: into using them to avert hold ups, to ward off car-jackers, frighten off suspected burglars by firing into the air, or going to the assistance of neighbours.

A number have been victims of shootings themselves, or have lost family members in hold ups that led to shootings.

Houses have fast been transformed into near fortresses through the measures that residents have taken to minimise burglaries, hold ups and theft from their yards. At least four striking features have become increasingly visible since 1995 *viz.* heightening of fences upon which spikes have been added, steel burglar guards around every window and door of the house, dogs trained to be vicious, and monitored alarm systems with armed responses by the monitoring company—at an added cost. Clare Estate and Reservoir Hills, among the middle class areas, and parts of Phoenix as the under-class area, especially those bordering the African townships of Kwa Mashu and Ntuzuma, were the major victims of spiralling squatter settlements. These suburbs have large tracts of unoccupied land, which have been an attraction to Africans who were affected by the violence or lack of space in the townships, or the sheer poverty in the rural areas. Their rapid rise has been greeted with ambiguous cries of sympathy or total opposition to their presence by the rates paying residents. To them the establishment of the squatter settlements was a mixture of sheer helplessness on the part of some and an aggressive response by others to the inability of the state to enforce control in the country. This actually amounted to land invasion of both private and state property. It radically altered the entire landscape of these areas, widely generated fear of walking on the streets alone—especially at night, and substantially reduced the value of property. Numerous attempts by residents to sell their houses either took years to do so or simply failed. Several homeowners were unable to emigrate because they could not sell their houses—which formed the major part of their transferable investments. Despite the predicament that the Indian residents in the middle class suburbs found themselves, their taxable property values remained the highest among the suburbs of Durban. This was brought about by the artificial shortage of land created through the 1950 Group Areas Act, which restricted Indians to minimal space for housing development.

However, the anxieties of the crime situation in places like Reservoir Hills and Clare Estate were no less in more built up and densely populated areas such as Asherville and Overport. Despite the significantly smaller and less visible number of squatter settlements in these areas, home protection measures were equally observable. There was widespread collaboration among the residents-especially in monitoring the squatter camps and forming vigilante groups to counter the rate of increasing burglaries and violent attacks against them and motorists. The formation of vigilante groups had to be under strict surveillance of the local police and they did not have any powers to make arrests. In Asherville and Overport the residents devised various strategies. However the Asherville group was more active than their Overport counterpart. Within single roads and smaller radiuses that incorporated several roads—covering more houses than the former—they either formed patrol groups or discussed ways in which they could operate more vigilantly without having to be out in the streets at night. The effectiveness of the patrol groups since they first began proved to be of tangible support to the residents. It significantly reduced burglaries and car-jackings and led to the arrest and conviction of numerous people. This success led to the vigilante groups becoming targets for the criminals who operated in the area. Several attacks took place against them, leading to a change in their tactics to patrol the area. Initially two cars made up of four males in each, each individual armed with one gun or more, split up and alternatively drove around and parked in strategic places throughout the night. At least four recorded attacks against these patrols took place. On two occasions they were shot at, at another stones were thrown at them and during the fourth attack people in two vehicles chased them until they were rescued by a passing police patrol. The attacks took place within a three-month period in 1997 although there was no evidence to suggest that this was the work of an individual or a single group. After they occurred the vigilantes felt compelled to increase their numbers by having a second car with four more armed individuals behind each leading patrol car. Their strategy has been to follow the leading car by a distance of at least one hundred metres in order to avoid detection as a team. No subsequent attacks took place after these events although the vigilantes did curtail more attempted burglaries, and they helped in the arrest of several thieves breaking into cars.

In areas where people did not feel the need to have patrolling vigilante groups but did feel the need to have at least a measure of vigilance, they formed cluster groups of ten or more houses. They periodically shared and exchanged information and collated their addresses and telephone numbers. During weekends and holidays when the occupants of a particular house went out for more than a night, all houses within the cluster were informed and were in a state of readiness for possible eventualities. The pattern of break-ins changed for a period late in 1997 when residents did not expect to be robbed. These attacks, at least five reported, occurred during the most unsuspecting times of the day. Three incidents happened on Sunday afternoons and two on weekday mornings between 10h00 and 12h00. One of the Sunday incidents occurred in Asherville when all the occupants of the house were gone out. A man casually walked into the yard at about 15h00 and attempted to enter the house by trying to climb through an open bathroom window that was neither visible from the road nor to the immediate neighbours. But in the process the owners had just returned and witnessed the incident. When they thought they had managed to subdue him, the burglar broke loose and started running. He was shot in the right leg and was arrested by the police. In another incident in Clare Estate a woman walked into the yard of a house at about 11h30 and casually started taking off the clothes from the lines. A ten old boy, alone with his granny at home while the rest of the family were out, witnessed this and thought that she was employed by the family, so he kept quiet not knowing that his clothes too for school the next day were being stolen.

Such incidents of theft from yards and houses have become a widespread phenomenon. Almost 60 per cent of the interviewees revealed information of such incidents, and almost inevitably they emphasised that it was "Africans" who were responsible. They consistently accused the state of failing in their duties to protect them and their properties and, therefore, find themselves in the situation of having to form vigilante groups—which although tolerated by the police—is not entirely welcome. Residents continually complained of the poorly ill-equipped and often apathetic South African Police Services, whose ability to execute their responsibilities with expectation has been frequently raised.

A Profile of the Interviewees from 1996 to 1998

Those interviewed were from diverse backgrounds and included males and females. They resided in the underclass township of Phoenix, and the middle class suburbs of Reservoir Hills, Clare Estate, Asherville, Overport, the Central Business District of Durban, as well as in the neighbouring towns of Verulam, Tongaat, Stanger and Umkoomaas. Additional interviews for comparative purposes were done in Cape

Town where there are substantially smaller Indian population and who are generally from middle-class to more affluent backgrounds.

Table 2.1: Reflecting basic information on 255 people interviewed from July 1997 to March 1999

Suburb	*Interviewees*	*Period of Interview*	*Males*	*Females*
Phoenix township	30	June, July, August 1997	22	8
Reservoir Hills Clare Estate Asherville Overport	120	July 1997; October-November 1997; July-November 1998	78	42
Central Durban	30	June, July, August 1997	18	12
Tongaat	15	April/May 1997	12	3
Stanger	15	January/February 1997	13	2
Umkoomaas	15	1997	11	4
Cape Town	30	November 1998	13	17

From Table 2.1 it is evident that one hundred and sixty-seven (167) of the interviewees were male and eighty-eight (88) were female. There was no deliberate intention to limit the number of females for interviews. The actual contact situation during fieldwork was dictated by several factors. At the workplaces such as in schools and in community based organisations such as in temples, those who were interviewed were the ones who were available, while at houses women often called males because they were either too shy to talk or their conservatism dictated that men should speak to strangers for any prolonged period. In the smaller towns of Tongaat, Stanger and Verulam conservatism was more pronounced and visible, while in the suburbs of Durban there was a greater tendency for women to either respond themselves or to participate in the interviews while their senior males were responding.

A number of conventional features with respect to Indian households still prevailed in the 1990s. For instance, the number who either resided in a single house or who occupied another abode in the same property were usually consistent with the conventional norms of extended or joint families. Both these structures, comprising of genealogical kin that in most cases consisted of three generation structures, have been common among people of Indian origin. The issue of joint and extended families are treated here as depicting different household structures. While the concept of the joint family is often used as an equivalent to the notion of extended family, its specific reference here is to indicate three generation households that is made up of patrilineal corporate groups where sons continue to reside with their parents after marriage. The dependencies between the two generations may vary according to earnings and resources at either generation's disposal. Extended family on the other hand is reference to a composite of domestic groups consisting of two or more nuclear families. Evidence for this project has limited such composites to married siblings and their nuclear families from patrilineal backgrounds. The persistence of this structure is generally for economic reasons. All working members of the household either pooled their earnings to allow the most senior person, either the patriarch or matriarch, to manage it, or each one assumed a monetary responsibility according to their earning capacities. This structure was also a platform from which siblings built up their capitals in order to eventually establish their own nuclear households.

While the economic reason is still the prevalent factor for the existence of extended and joint households, the contemporary political climate was the first reason to be attributed for its continuation. In the middle-class suburbs where second and third generation individuals have been unable to amass sufficient funds to purchase houses, their reasons to remain in their natal households were socio-political. Respondents generally felt that the political climate for investing in real estate in South Africa was too risky, and that for young couples to be purchasing properties while both are employed, is impractical and dangerous in view of the extent of burglaries. The latter reason has often been the first and most widely cited explanation for the retention of conventional household patterns. Expressions such as *"It's too dangerous and inconvenient to let our children buy their own houses in this day and age"* and *"Properties are too expensive to invest in right now when our future as Indians in this country is so dicy"*, have been made varyingly in every interview that presented such a scenario. From the 255 interviews mentioned above, 163 of the individuals came from three-generation households. While there was interestingly varying structures across the number of three-generation households, not all of them could have been followed up for more detailed information. Of the 163, 120 interviews were done out in Overport, Clare Estate, Reservoir Hills and Asherville, out of which 73 belonged to three-generation structures. Variations of this structure were at least four-fold *viz.*

1. Being part of a single unit where all cooked, ate and shared responsibilities collectively;
2. Extended the existing structure to accommodate the growing family of younger sons permitting a measure of autonomy but still collectively engaging in household responsibilities;
3. Extending the existing structure to build an independent unit including a separate entrance and kitchen, whereby the financial responsibilities become more distinctly demarcated.
4. Building or renovating an independent structure on the property in order to acquire a measure of independence, but like the above having expenditure more distinctly demarcated.

Table 2.2 provides a breakdown of the 73 households from Overport, Clare Estate, Reservoir Hills and Asherville.

Table 2.2: Depicting number of joint/extended household type where each number represents the corresponding type mentioned in the four-fold depiction immediately above

1	*2*	*3*	*4*
23	18	17	15

Most of the 73 households depicted above considered the joint or extended family situation as an unquestionable phenomenon. Discussion about the situation sometimes made it difficult for the respondents to try and understand why this presented such a curiosity. The responsibilities that parents or grand-parents felt about keeping their kin either in the same yard or under the same roof was articulated as a moral and cultural one. It was presented as a norm that would have made any deviation from this totally unacceptable either to parents, children or grand-children. Normative kinship responsibilities requires parents to shield children and grand-children up to a point until they are sufficiently independent to set up homes of their own. The reciprocal expectation is to ensure that elderly members of the household are cared for by immediate kin and not relegated to old age homes.

The feeling to reciprocate care was generally mutual among young and old although more direct hints from at least two daughters-in-law intimated that such situations are neither the ideal nor preferable. Such daughters-in-law felt strongly about living on their own as nuclear households but were only willing to succumb to such circumstances because their spouses felt they had a responsibility towards their elders. When the opportunities arose for them to express their dissatisfaction with their living arrangements during the interviews, they either hinted at the inconveniences or gestured in disapproving ways to get their spouses attention. One commented "But the house is fully burglar guarded, it has a monitored alarm and the neighbours are reliable. Although there have been break-ins in the area, this is a generally safe area. I think we will appreciate each other more if we live on our own". In the second incident a woman expressively and cynically retorted when her spouse stated that he would not leave his parents to live on his own because of their vulnerability to attack: "Hmmm, how now nice eh? Where are the attacks coming from and who is the daily victim here?" Not surprisingly both women were full time housewives who were in the continuous company of their husbands' parents.

Most wives however presented an impression of having resigned to their fates in joint and extended household situations. Their preferences were not always openly expressed. Despite the independence that many wives have acquired through their professions and personalities, they generally felt inclined to follow the normative pattern in household structure and their spouses' feelings of obligations towards their parents or grand-parents. There was often an expressed obligation to reciprocate care and the difficulties of breaking affinal bondage in tightly knit households. Likewise, there was an expressed need to cluster together as family in a climate of fear, economic instability and to ensure survival of cultural norms. At least twenty of the women who participated in the interviews were positively expressive about living in joint/extended household situations. They were all professional or working women who enjoyed at least one or more of the following common benefits:

- caring for children who do not go to school,
- taking and picking up children from school,
- caring for them thereafter,
- cooking and keeping the kitchen clean,
- laundering and ironing clothes, and
- general administration of household care through the employment of maids, gardeners and odd job employees.

The benefits in these cases outweighed the disadvantages and the women communicated this as though they have been the major benefactors. One of the respondents, from a mother of two children aged four and eighteen months, replied in these words: "You know, having my in-laws at home is such a blessing. My father-in-law takes my children for walks during the day and buys everything we need for the house when it's necessary. He takes them shopping with my mother-in-law and breaks their boredom during the day. My mother-in-law baths and changes the children and cooks the food. She also sees to the duties of the maid. When I come home tired in the evenings there is very little for me to do. I just eat, enjoy my children and the clean house. After having lived on our own for a while, I really appreciate this set-up. If I live on my own I'll die!"

The high frequency of joint families required a more in-depth examination into the lifestyles of the respondents. An arbitrary figure of twenty was selected to acquire detailed information and life histories from among the bigger pool of respondents.

Table 2.3 illustrates the variations in household sizes, occupations of the first and second generations in the households, the number of kin who make up the household, their combined earnings, and the domestic assistants they employ. It is apparent from the evidence that joint households are greater in number than the extended households. The latter however, were originally joint households as well, but became extended households after the deaths of the first generations. The diversity of their occupations and their combined incomes are indications of their relatively well off economic positions. The amount of R5000.00 was based on the cut-off point used by banks and building societies which calculate home loan repayments of up to R2000.00 per month and basic living expenses for a family of seven to be in the region of +R2500.00 per month. Everyone of the households had incomes that exceeded the amount of R5000.00. All of them had displayed situations of relative comfort and did not indicate any desperate need to transcend their contemporary earnings. The homes were well furnished and curtained and the yards and houses were sufficiently spacious to accommodate the number living in each home. Five of the twenty houses did not have domestic maids. In four of the cases there was an expressed desire to take responsibility for their own household duties. In one case the practice had stopped because the maid was allegedly responsible for setting up a burglary in the house. In all five cases domestic work was associated with the

Table 2.3: Depicting information on seven issues from 20 households

Household type	*Previous occupation of retired couple*	*Occupation of second generation*	*House size by number of bedrooms*	*Household number*	*Joint income, in excess of R5000.00*	*Domestic assistants*
1. Joint	Clerical; housewife	Teacher; Bank	4	6	Yes	Yes
2. Joint	School principal; housewife	Lawyer; University lecturer	5	8	Yes	Yes
3. Joint	Bus owner; housewife	Mechanic; Hotel receptionist	4	5* *no third generation*	Yes	Yes
4. Joint	Teacher; Teacher	Bank; teacher	6	9	Yes	Yes
5. Joint	Insurance; housewife	Computer analyst; housewife	4	7	Yes	Yes
6. Joint	Electrical contractor; housewife	Electrical contractor; teacher	6	8	Yes	Yes
7. Joint	Owner: printing press; assistant	Printing press; assistant	5	6	Yes	Yes
8. Joint	Truck driver; housewife	Welder; Doctor's surgery	5	8	Yes	No
9. Joint	Deceased; housewife	Dentist; attorney	4	5	Yes	Yes
10. Joint	Deceased; housewife	Teacher; Teacher	5	6	Yes	Yes
11. Joint	Deceased	Bus owner; hotel receptionist	7	8* *four generations*	Yes	No
12. Joint	Teacher; housewife	Computer technician; housewife	4	5	Yes	Yes
13. Joint	Insurance agent; teacher	Doctor; physio-therapist	5	5	Yes	Yes
14. Joint	Deceased; housewife	Butcher; housewife	7	10	Yes* *two maids—own and common entrances*	Yes
15. Joint	Truck owner; housewife	Clerical-with "retired" father	6	11	Yes	Yes
16. Joint	Deceased; housewife	Attornney; attorney	4	4	Yes	No
17. Joint	Supermarket owner; housewife	Optometrist; pharmacist	7	6* *no third generation*	Yes	Yes
18. Extended	—	Vegetable vendors; school assistant; school secretary	6	9	Yes	No
19. Extended	—	Bus owners; hotel receptionist	6	8	Yes	No
20. Extended	—	Garage owners	8	12	Yes	Yes

employment of African women, for whom there was a distinct aversion because of mistrust and the association of burglaries with African men. The domestic responsibilities were generally understood as a gender based responsibility and were carried out by the women of the houses while men usually saw to the gardening. However, the latter activity was often done through the part time employment of gardeners, who were mainly "trusted African" males. There was profound emphasis on this issue, which was linked to the political climate and the perceptions that so many residents spoke about as a necessity. The screening of part time gardeners and their familiarity either to members within the household or to some other known person of the household was a crucial factor in the employment of the "trusted African male". Such fear emanates from an allegedly high record of attacks by gardeners who have been employed without the householders checking their credentials, as well as attacks by those who have been employed for a longer period[4].

Despite the generally large sizes of the households domestic cleaning and gardening had become too menial, too tiring to do or just not possible with the time they had at their disposal. There was a distinct division of labour that was either gender or racially based. In most cases their middle class statuses afforded them the opportunities to employ full time or part time maids or gardeners.

An Analysis of the Responses

Almost inevitably the interviews and periods of participant observation turned into *laissez-faire* conversations about the fear psychosis that prevailed so soon after the first democratic general elections in South Africa. The open-ended nature of the questionnaire induced such conversations and they became unavoidable to entertain. Often, it was in these discourses that the unanimous feelings or differences within the households, about the nature and pace of change, emerged. Each questionnaire comprised of a basic outline of 22 questions, many of which produced answers that required follow-up questions. For instance, when respondents commented on either the negative or positive changes, which they thought occurred after the election, their replies provoked additional questions. From the 255 respondents to these questions, 171 responded with outright condemnation of the South African government. From the remaining 84, 58 of the respondents were ambivalent about change while the remaining 26 were positive about the future.

The most common replies to the positive changes from the positive respondents were:

- Repeal of the 1950 Group Areas Act, which permits people to purchase homes in areas of their choice,
- Promotion of a human rights culture,
- Freedom of speech,
- Freedom of movement,
- The right to vote without reference to race,
- The right to marry a partner of one's choice,
- Freedom to communicate with people of other race groups,
- Increased investments from overseas,
- Better opportunities for Indians through affirmative action,
- The right to join a political party of one's choice,
- Evidence of Indian Cabinet Ministers who fought against the apartheid government, and
- Increased, improved and legitimate communication with India.

Those who were negative and ambivalent about the future of South Africa were in the majority and they mainly produced the inverse of the responses above, although several of them did allude to some of these answers as well. Their despondency was more complex than the variations of the answers that centered on the violence that so many had spoken about. The negative issues ranged from strong belief in a situation of disorder and chaos (most negative) to manageable issues of control and hope over time (the ambivalent):

- No positive change at all and unlikely to occur,
- The country is going the same route as the rest of Africa,
- Uncontrollable violence and inability of businesses to function normally because of hold-ups,
- Increasing costs of home and business security measures,
- Rapid increase in car-jacking and car theft,
- Inability of the state to control crime,
- Lack of ability and willingness on the part of the state to deal with criminals effectively,
- Drop in the standards of education but an increase in its costs,
- Inability of the state to provide housing and employment,
- Drop in health standards and deteriorating conditions in state hospitals,

- Affirmative action being selectively employed for benefit of Africans at the expense of Indians and Coloureds,[5]
- Rising cost of living,
- Increasing belligerence by taxi operators and the inability of the police to contain their violent behavior and lack of discipline on the roads,
- The rapid increase in vigilante groups because of the ineffectiveness of the police—many of whom lack training or who enter into the forum with preconceived racist notions,
- The state's lack of vision to produce a meaningful programme of action to boost development and confidence in the future of the country, considering the failure of the Reconstruction and Development Plan (RDP) and the introduction of the controversial Growth, Economic and Redistribution Plan (GERP), and
- Lack of overseas investor confidence because of the problems listed above.

Both sets of positive and negative comments allude to the contemporary feelings of hope, fears and anxieties of the respondents. What they have been articulating in the interviews, public meetings, and one on one conversations and social gatherings are important reflections of how people of Indian origin feel about transformation in post-apartheid South Africa. In the set of positive comments 83 people deliberately chose to speak in non-racial terms. Forty-seven of the 83 responded by emphatically denouncing the label of "Indian" with reference to themselves, while the remaining 36 put their South African origin before that of their Indian origin. They preferred to avoid the label "Indian", but were not totally averse to it being used in describing them. But it had to follow a particular order. They were emphatic, if the word Indian had to be used, that they were first referred to as "South African Indians" and not *vice versa.* An important political statement was made in this manner of emphasis in that their South African identities had to receive priority before their Indian identities. Their general defence of this position was that they were born and bred South Africans with no Indian identity other than that of their ancestral backgrounds. For this reason their positions as South Africans were unique and not easily comparable with their counterparts on the Indian sub-continent or with Indians in other countries. They often commented on those who preferred to see themselves as "Indians", viewing them as actually denying or being ignorant of their real identities. These respondents were generally aware of the political world, very articulate and hopeful for the future of the country. They did not associate the turmoil in other African countries with the present lack of direction that so many others believe to be the major problem in South Africa. The general feeling among these respondents was that the population at large should understand the constraints under which the state is operating and it is, therefore, unable to deliver services and correct the imbalances of the past as swiftly as people would like. This was despite the fact that the ANC, before being elected into government, themselves created expectations by making promises such as creation of jobs, building one million houses in five years, free education and improved health facilities.

An assertive respondent, who insisted on being called South African, was a civic leader and a staunch supporter of the ANC. He grew in popularity for challenging the Durban City Council for the high taxes they charged property owners in predominantly Indian residential areas (previously Indian Group Areas). But he lost favour with a number of Indian residents for ingratiating himself with neighbouring African squatters. While he publicly defended the existence of African squatter camps he also fought against over rated Indian properties as a matter of principle, because during apartheid they were overvalued and, therefore, over taxed. This was a result of the artificial shortage of land created through the 1950 Group Areas Act. He saw his role as being one of reconciliation between Indians and Africans. The problem in his area was the increasing rise in crime, resulting in tension between the Indian residents and African squatters. He remarked: "A number of Indians do not like the fact that there is now a Black majority government in place. Some of them who are unhappy are doing the right thing and leaving the country while others are continuously moping about the slow pace of change and delivery. Many of them see crime as an African phenomenon, but they don't see how many Indians for instance are dealing with drugs and going to India to bring thousands of rands worth of mandrax! What about the violence and lawlessness in these acts?.... When it comes to delivery for the whole country everybody must realise that it is going to take a very long time to undo the effects of apartheid.... And the Africans too must realise that they must start paying up for the services they get, otherwise it won't be long before the local municipalities run bankrupt. Maybe on this score the Indians have a better track record than the Africans—but they must also understand their (Africans) history too".

Another equally popular ANC supporter, a teacher[6] in Phoenix township, withdrew his support for the party and became ambivalent about the future of the country. He had a long history of mobilising to change old mindsets and increase membership for the ANC during apartheid among the township residents. But events since their takeover after the April 1994 general election led him to seriously rethink his support for them after two stabbing incidents. One of them was fatal which led to him having to flee his school and go into hiding for several weeks. While he maintained that he was South African before any other designation such as "Indian" was assigned to him, he was losing faith in the future of the country and of the ability of the ANC to govern it and address legitimate minority issues. He taught in a school that had 60 per cent and 40 per cent Indian and African pupils respectively. In a room in which he arranged for himself and seven other teachers to be interviewed as a group, an impressive range of posters were pasted on all the walls. The posters were graphic illustrations against AIDs, sexual control, responsibilities of the pupils in the classroom, advice against vandalism, a picture of President Nelson Mandela as well as a picture of the new South African flag, the importance of recognising the multi-cultural nature of South African society, career opportunities and a copy of the new constitution. About the posters on the wall, he commented: "Becoming a multi-cultural teacher first means becoming a multi-cultural person. We need to learn more about ourselves, confront our own racism and biases, and learn to see reality from a variety of perspectives. I thought the ANC was going to promote this sort of culture. But the changes they have effected are on a superficial level only. We probably have one of the best constitutions in the world, but there is little else to it. The ANC's failure to control crime and deal with criminals effectively, and live up to the expectations it created, led to it being trounced in the local government elections in 1996. In Chatsworth it lost to the Minority Front and in Phoenix it lost to the National Party—which is a disgrace for a party that has such huge support in the African areas. I really did not get much support from the party big wigs during the elections when I was neither mobilising for them nor when I was in trouble during the stabbing incidents. They would not have done the same thing in an important African constituency if a by-election were to take place there.

So why should I bother anymore about them?" The teacher's serious rethink about his support for the ANC and his shift from "South African" to "South African Indian" began when an Indian pupil in his school was allegedly stabbed by an African pupil. A few days later, uniformed African pupils stabbed to death a twenty-five-year old unemployed Indian man who went to fetch his nephew after school. The neighbouring Indian community, described by a parent as generally apathetic, suddenly vociferously galvanised in what appeared to be a knee-jerk reaction. Indian parents demanded that African pupils be removed from the school. For several days after the murder they gathered outside the gate shouting: "We don't want Blacks here!" The police were forced to stop people from entering the school until the tension was reduced to safer levels. The community also viewed the teacher under discussion as being the main perpetrator since he fought a sustained battle to have his school integrated into a non-racial one. Community anger against Africans led to a segment of mobilised members to turn against all the Africans who passed through their area. The first attack led to the stabbing of an innocent African worker who was passing through the area after work—who was saved by the police. The *Daily News* (March 6, 1997) presented a front-page colour photograph of the victim with a torn blood splattered shirt, adding that teacher (mentioned above), was also threatened by angry community members for trying to force integration in the school. This led him to abandon his leadership role in the area for the ANC, but he claimed that he would still work independently towards racial harmony in the country. For the first time he thought seriously about emigration, but felt stifled by the thought of having to start life all over again in a foreign country. However, he vowed to leave South Africa if he had enough money to do so. This was echoed by his other colleagues in the group interview. Their main reason for remaining in South Africa was financial and their common reasons for wanting to emigrate was lawlessness, corruption and a generally bleak future for the country. They however conditioned themselves to think positively about the future despite the realities by which they are confronted, in order, as one of them stated, *"to keep our sanity"*.

On the contrary, the 172 respondents who preferred seeing themselves first as "Indians" were doing so for several reasons. Among many of these respondents there was still a high degree of continuity from the apartheid era with reference to their identities, when circumstances conditioned them to think of themselves as an ethnic category *i.e.* "Indians". In numerous instances, such reference was made in innocence and in ignorance of the more recent efforts by the state to build a national consciousness that is free from the ethnic labelling of the past. Such individuals tended to determine their identities on the basis of their religious beliefs and practices, their eating habits and their general exposure to mainly people of Indian origin during apartheid. Their indoctrination during this period, brought about as a result of the insular effects of the 1950 Group Areas Act, has kept them adamant about maintaining such an identity. The response in this issue was often coupled with reference to their pride in their ancestral homeland *i.e.* India, and to the way in which Indians in general will be viewed as a minority in South Africa irrespective of what the state might propagate. They demonstrated a strong tendency to view politics in ethnic terms and a tacit to overt pronouncement that politics will always be ethnically based. One elderly male respondent, a retired school principal, retorted on the issue in these words: "What difference will it make despite what the state says it is doing to create a culture of non-racialism? The fact that they are targeting Africans in the job market at the expense of capable Indians, is proof of the inconsistencies in the new South Africa. The African government is trying to do what the National Party did for the Afrikaners from 1948. But I must warn you they are incapable of doing the same for their own people. As a former school principal, I must tell you that education as we received it through the Department of Indian Affairs is going to be like a dream very soon. There are already signs of the system cracking by encouraging the best people to resign by offering them packages. The African has got no experience in the administration of education and they are sure to make a mess of it. I know what the quality of teaching is in those schools—my brother is an inspector of schools and he goes to the African townships from time to time. The teachers don't really care there. We were much better off under the White man!"

There was a visible degree of belligerence among most of these 172 respondents because of the ways in which their lives have actually been affected by transformation. Several factors were common in most of their experiences, including being

- burgled,
- car-jacked,
- held up at home or in the family business,
- mugged in the street,

- a relative of murdered person through a hold-up or violent confrontation,
- victims of theft of clothes, children's toys or other household belongings stolen from the yard, theft of cars,
- victims of devalued properties by living close to a squatter camps and not being able to sell their property,
- victims of overcrowded schools with second language children from African based squatter camps, forcing them to send children to schools outside their suburbs at phenomenally higher costs—especially in predominantly White suburbs where good management, control and discipline are still in tact,
- victim of affirmative action, and
- not being able to continue with normal social life in the evenings and nights because of the security factor.

The issues highlighted above are represented in Table 2.4, outlining the incidents to which the interviewees and their household members had fallen victim. A number of individuals and households have been affected by more than one incident. The impact in each case brought the overwhelming majority of respondents to view life in South Africa in terms of their experiences.

Table 2.4: Illustrating the issue by which the 172 respondents were affected—either personally or by a family member being a victim

Issue	*Number*
Burglary	68
Car-jacking	53
Hold-up in home	58
Held up in business	26
Mugged in the street	17
Murder	15
Theft of household belongings	112
Property devaluation	132
Inability to sell property	37
Living close to squatter camp	56
Choosing a school outside the suburb	102
Affirmative action	85
No/reduced social life	151

In each category listed in Table 2.4 above the descriptions and traumatic experiences that the respondents underwent are too vast and varied to incorporate here. There was widespread unapologetic nostalgia about the rule of law and relative peace that existed during the previous White dominated government of the National Party. In at least 173 out of the total of 255 interviews, variations of a common sentiment were made: "At least under the White government we could walk the streets peacefully", or "Under the White government crime and corruption was controllable". From the 172 respondents who are represented in Table 2.4, 77 of them experienced two or more incidents either in their homes, businesses, in the streets or at work. The common incidents, as reflected in the table, were thefts and the devaluation of property. There has been a variety of ways in which personal and household property has been lost. The most frequent occurrence that has been reported was theft of washed clothes drying on the outside lines and to a lesser extent children's toys that were left outside.

The 68 burglaries, 58 hold-ups in the homes and 26 hold-ups in the businesses recorded losses and experiences that ranged from mild physical attacks to severe damages to property and life. The burglaries that were recorded were of three types *viz.* in the absence of the householders, while they were either unaware that the incident was taking during the day or at night while they were asleep. To this extent the burglaries were non-violent attacks in that householders were not physically harmed, although the damage to their houses and financial standing was serious in several cases. In at least seven cases the household contents were either not or inadequately insured and their losses ranged from approximately R1000.00 to R150,000.00. In the former cases, which were four, video machines, televisions, car radios, stereo sets and tools, including lawn mowers, were stolen. In the bigger burglaries the maids were the first to be blamed—accused of either willingly or under pressure—supplying the burglars with information. Of the three who were affected by bigger losses, all blamed their maids for the occurrences. Their evidence was cited by the fact that their maids either did not return to work or was acting suspiciously after the incidents. Two of three were not insured at all, while the third was insured for only a fraction of what was lost. The estimated amounts of R40,000.00, R65,000.00 and R150,000.00 were recorded respectively. The victim, indicated by the last amount, had insured his household contents to the value of R90,000.00 only. He did not include his furniture, which was also stolen and given an estimated value of R60,000.00. He claimed: "My house was completely wiped out when we went to the Wild Coast Casino in December last year (1998) for three nights. By the second night I had to break away with my family from the rest of my group and go back home.... I can't tell you how much my wife cried for the next week and how little sleep we had for the next few months. Our house became a nightmare to us—we didn't feel like we owned it anymore".

In the 26 business hold-ups, seven of them occurred between 8h30 and 10h00 when only women were present, 5 occurred early in the morning when the business was just being opened between 06h00 and 07h00, and the remaining 14 occurred in different times of the day. Home made guns were allegedly used in 2 robberies, while in other cases regular pistols, knives, choppers and sticks were used. In 4 of these cases, 4 members of the households were killed through shooting, 8 were injured through either shooting, stabbing or been beaten with a variety of weapons or through being punched, kicked or banged against the walls. In 3 cases the robbers were shot dead by the owners, in 4 cases they were shot dead by the police, and in 2 cases arrests of a total of 6 were made.

The other issues relating to devaluation of and inability to sell properties because of the squatter problems, choosing new schools for children and affirmative action are amplified in the chapters that follow. Against the background of such experiences respondents were only too eager to articulate their frustrations in terms of their unpleasant experiences and the growing lack of morale in the country, impacting severely on their perceptions about future socio-political scenarios.

Some Predominant Socio-Political Trends

A major component in tea-room gossips, socialisation among friends, "street corner" conversations and weekend family based social gatherings is the predominance of discussion on the nature of transformation in post-apartheid South Africa. Inevitably the issues that are depicted in Table 2.4 acquire prominence. It is because of the extent to which this is occurring throughout the country that the media coverage it is receiving is so widespread. The conversations in any one scenario often:

- elicited strong positive views on the recent past of White dominated rule and intense debates on the nature and pace of change,
- induced talk on negative effects of affirmative action—especially where under-qualified Africans are being favoured,
- got people hoping about the manner in which voting for the

1999 general elections was likely to take place—most frequently in the hope that the ANC was to substantially reduce or lose its support base,
- the preferred political choices, and
- heard yearnings and dreams to flee the country with adequate bank balances.

In respect of these factors, transformation has become synonymous with corruption, inability to govern effectively, a lack of state vision, violence, car-jacking, bank robberies and a time to emigrate. In the same vein social gatherings have become synonymous with a time to talk about these problems. The newspapers abound with these headlines on a daily basis: **"Indian fears misplaced, says Mandela"** (*Daily News*, October 28, 1998), **"Community (Indian) living in fear"** (*Sunday Tribune Herald*, August 9, 1998), **"Freeze, flee...or fight"** (*Sunday Tribune Herald*, August 16, 1998), **"The killing goes on..."** (*Highway Mail*, November 14, 1997), **"Crime stats queried—figures don't add up, say the experts"** (the *Saturday Paper*, February 14, 1998). The first two headlines that are quoted had opening paragraphs that were consistent with the ethnographic information that is presented above. For instance, the first report opened with the following words: "Crime, affirmative action, education and unemployment were some of the concerns and fears raised by Lotus FM listeners yesterday when they were given a chance to question President Nelson Mandela." The other started off with these words: "There are three physiological responses, which every animal displays when it is in a state of fear: it freezes, flees or turns to fight. Now, if there is one characteristic that defines the Indian community in South Africa it is fear, as expected, it responds as the way nature decrees". Several newspapers have also reported on the extent to which conversations on the negative aspects of transformation in social gatherings have become an unavoidable aspect. People now address the issues with virtual obsession about the state of the nation.

This has had significant effects on evening and late night socialisation. Most of the respondents have developed an aversion to socialise during these hours because of the dangers such as being car-jacked, shot at or robbed. One person commented: "You just have to drive out after seven at night and you'll find the streets deserted. You'll only find Africans roaming the streets after this hour. If you are alone walking in the streets you are sure to be attacked. So many people have been hijacked at robots at night that it is now too dangerous to be out. If we do go out it is always more than one person, or we make sure that we are not out too late. Because then you don't know who's waiting to attack you in your yard."

The types of crime that are spoken about here are generally associated with Africans. These areas have been middle class Indian Group Areas during apartheid and as settled tax paying residents the people have been forced to coexist with African squatters who have been branded as land invaders. The latter's poverty stricken situation has bred among them a number of criminals who have considered stealing their only way to transcend their marginalised existences. And the victims in these areas are usually people of Indian origin—whose insulated lives have done little to inform them about the extent to which innocent Africans become victims of African thugs as well. In an interview with an Indian tuck-shop operator who relied on business from neighbouring African squatters, he related an eye-witness account of a street mugging: "People think only Indians are victims. But last Tuesday I saw an Indian guy walk past about eleven o'clock at night. These two African guys left him and attacked the other African guy walking behind him. They stabbed him twice, took his wallet and finished him on the floor. The poor guy's clothes were all torn, and they even stole his shoes."

Conclusion

The perception on the ground, which influences the socio-political trend, is thus pervasively ethnically and racially scarred. There is common mistrust among both Africans and Indians, who generally loathe their forced coexistence as people of significantly varying means. A careful analysis of both segments will reveal that their differences cannot be simplistically viewed either along racial or class lines. The perceptions are not just a creation and continuity of the apartheid era but are powerful reminders of the mistrust between ethnic and racial categories that has risen to the fore at a frighteningly accelerated pace throughout the world in the 1990s. The state's handling of racial mistrust is to date a virtual denial of the realities on the ground. A part of the empowerment process for the disadvantaged Africans has been to accept their land invasion on privately owned properties, thereby widening the schism between Indian landowners and impoverished Africans. The divide is rooted in Indian ownership, African invasion and municipality tolerance. In the all of the research areas, besides Phoenix, the most visible signs of differences are actually class based.

While Indians live in solidly structured brick and tile houses with carefully landscaped gardens, Africans are crammed together in nearby small empty spaces of land that is saturated with houses built out of cardboard, timber, masonite boards and plastic that are unlikely to withstand prolonged spells of inclement weather conditions. Social services in the form of electricity, sanitation and water supply, are the privileges of only those who are legally occupying property and who are the ones who have the means to afford it.

However, the endemic levels of crime are re-entrenching the racial perceptions of the past. It has eroded the euphoria, nascent racial trust and hope that characterised the pre-election period of April 1994. Police and media records, as well as interviewee responses indicate that in the research areas Indians are the victims and Africans make up the majority of the criminals. Out of this emerges a situation that is more race-based than class based. Most Indians however are not adequately schooled in the history of class development and racial privileges in South Africa and are, therefore, not able to conceptualise the associated problems in terms other than with ethnic or racial dimensions. This is a major preoccupation in people's spare time and is further elucidated in the chapters that follow.

REFERENCES

1. Immediately after the general election a Government of National Unity was formed, incorporating all the major political parties in the running of the state.
2. Towards the latter part of 1995 the levels of political violence in most affected areas in the country had subsided. But other forms of violence through escalating criminal activity were replacing it.
3. Interview with Inspector Vinesh Singh, Sydenhm Police Station, 1 March 1999. The figures for 1995 were not available at the time of interview.
4. Attempts at acquiring statistics on this issue from the police public relations sector were unsuccessful. The reason was that such crime was recorded under general categories of assault, murder, burglaries etc.
5. According to the state decree on affirmative action Africans, Colored and Indians are considered as disadvantaged and therefore should be considered on equal terms for employment.
6. Interviewed on 24/6/1997, 26/6/1997 and 30/7/1997. The first interview was a result of a leading front-page article in the *Daily News* 6 March 1997, with a colour photograph of a bleeding African worker and a story of the violence between Indians and Africans in the interviewee's school.

CHAPTER THREE

Residents' Perceptions of Informal Settlements: The Situation in Clare Estate

Introduction

> "*When South Africa got its freedom this year the Indians lost theirs*".
>
> "*This district is finished. It's gone to the dogs*".

The quotations above are characteristic of the type of conversations that residents of Clare Estate engaged in regularly. They surfaced on a blistering hot mid-day conversation, at a house where the funeral of a seventy-four year old pioneer resident of the area was taking place. As family members sat in mourning around the body that lay in state, guests and relatives sat under a marquee tent and gathered under shady trees observing with the curiosity of very disturbed minds—the movements of occupants from the sprawling informal settlement across the road. The sadness of the occasion was exacerbated by a tension in the atmosphere that was cast by a recently foiled robbery in the corner store opposite the bereaved family's house. At 09h00 on the Sunday before the day of the funeral there was hold-up in the store by three armed men, one of who had a loaded pistol. Before they could make off with their loot the police arrived, surrounded the shop and shot two of the three suspects, killing one of them and wounding another. A shop assistant was also shot and killed in the crossfire. In the confusion the third suspect managed to escape into the informal settlement with the cash box of the shop's till. While I was ever mindful of the fact that I was attending a funeral, my curiosity and interest in the Clare Estate residents perceptions of the sprouting of informal settlements in the area urged me to make mental notes. I moved within the space of about half an hour to several little gatherings at the funeral, to greet many long lost friends. At each little gathering, as I rightly guessed, the conversations were about informal settlements, security, and the situation in a transforming Black dominated South Africa. At least one comment appeared to have fused the occasion to our wider surroundings. The remark was made as a gesture of insecurity, by a person mindful of his minority status and out of sheer frustration with the problems of crime and informal settlements: *"Mr. Harribaran was born and brought up in Clare Estate and he helped to build it up with pride from nothing. He is now going to rest in peace while we see these people tear everything down".*

Clare Estate is one of Durban's northern suburbs, which, during the years of apartheid was earmarked for Indian occupation only. Homes are privately owned by people who work in the civil service, as petty entrepreneurs, and as legal and medical professionals. Amidst the undulating and scenic landscape individually architectured homes are a prominent feature. Most roads are well constructed with asphalt and are flanked by elevated pavements on both sides. Most of the homes are surrounded by an average of one metre high concrete fencing within which are relatively well-laid out gardens. They are situated on plots of sloping land that averages about one thousand square metres. In the road facing part of the homeowners' yards or the entrances to their homes emblems such as red flags swaying high on bamboo or aluminium poles, flowers strung across the top of front doorways, or writings in Arabic, English, Sanskrit or other variations of the Indian dialects, serve as distinctive ethnic, religious or linguistic markers. Despite the diversity of the religious and linguistic backgrounds the Group Areas Act of 1950 had encouraged the residents of Clare Estate to mould among themselves an image of "Indianness". There was never really a need to collectively and publicly assert this image over a sustained period. However, since 1991, when the unbridled proliferation of squatters in Clare Estate besieged their residents, a collective and assertive community consciousness has been enforced upon them. The biggest among them, with more than 30,000 people squeezed within one square kilometre, was given a name with Biblical origins, Canaan (promised land). Its origins, magnitude and perceived threat to the lives and property of Clare Estate's residents made an in-depth analysis of the settlement unavoidable.

A Brief Insight to Canaan

Canaan's history is rooted in the apartheid era when Africans were criminalised for finding employment and shelter without permits in South Africa's urban and industrial areas. The settlement conjures up images of other sprawling shack settlements in Durban's Cato Manor in the 1940s, where the policies of the White dominated government were put through substantial strains and tests by its African occupants. Makhatini's (1994) case study of the resuscitated shack settlement in Cato Manor in the 1990s is a descriptive account of how it developed and by who it was inhabited. The authorities have built up a reputation for not providing housing within the time limits it proposed to provide for the shack dwellers, and neither did it provide services for them when they needed it most (Makhatini, 1994: 63). Cato Monor has a history of dynamic and volatile relationships between Indian residents and African squatters, as Edwards and Nuttal's (1990) instrumenatlist analysis reveals. Their paper on the riots in 1949 between Indians and Africans revealed the disparities that led to the tension and violent clashes between Africans and Indians. Similarly, Hindson and Byerly's (1993) report on a survey of households in Canaan squatter camp, reveals tremendous disparities between Indian residents and African squatters in the early 1990s. However, their conclusions about the relationships of the people in the squatter camp and Clare Estate are paradoxically different from the information that was collected for this chapter. Their presentation, being tabulated representations to questions of their survey undertaken in April-May 1993, with a few lines commentary under each table, lacked any clarity on their methodology and analysis of their data. In commenting on the responses to the question *"What is the nature of the relationship between people in this area and Clare Estate?"* they wrote: "From the responses it seems that residents of Canaan felt that relationships between the two areas were good." Such a comment can only be derived from an impersonal approach to the research and a lack of comparative responses from the Indian residents themselves. My approach to understanding the responses from residents to the squatters was a long drawn out qualitative process that spanned over several months and with people from both sides.

In March 1993, for reasons other than this research, I managed to trace an individual who was identified as a pioneering resident in Canaan. A doctor I used to help on Sunday mornings as a paramedic for a mobile clinic set up by a religious body, the Ramakrishna Centre of South Africa, introduced him to me. His name was Amos, and was described as "a man who lived all his life by his wits alone". Our involvement in the clinic was voluntary. The residents' appreciation of this made my task of gathering information a lot easier. At the time of the interview Amos was a fifty-three years old single parent with a two years old daughter. He was a willing respondent who found it neither tiresome nor burdensome to divulge information about his history or events in the settlement. Amos retraced the history of Canaan to a period in 1987, when he was invited by a friend to build a shack for himself in an area he considered safe, later to be called Canaan. Up to 1987 Amos recalled that he made a successful living in Central Durban as a squatter. But the political situation then, under P.W. Botha's reign, was becoming increasingly tense and led to the evacuation of all squatters from South Africa's city centres. The process was justified by the state as a necessary security precaution. Moving from place to place daily and living under constant fear of the security forces, Amos agreed to his friend's invitation.

In that period squatting in residential areas was totally forbidden. Mindful of this, Amos, like his friend built what they allegedly referred to as a "dog shack". This structure was an ingenious way of eluding the police and public by making sure that it was not visible from the road. It was built up to a height that was lower than the long savannah type grass that grew in the area, just big enough to accommodate sleeping space for one individual. Amos recalled that as African anger against apartheid intensified and people were no longer prepared to return to either the troubled townships or the impoverished rural areas, they became more resilient and began building more "dog shacks". As their numbers grew and the reign of P.W. Botha was being evidently increasingly challenged and loosened, people began building bigger shacks. Eventually the large numbers in Canaan and in nearby informal settlements generated a measure of solidarity that encouraged them to build more solid and bigger structures, which in many instances have grown to include two rooms and a kitchen.

Amos was quite enterprising in the art of building shack dwellings. From his meagre knowledge in carpentry skills he learnt some cost-effective ways of building shacks and earning a living. He collected most of his building materials from a nearby dump, which became an indispensable resource for many residents in Canaan. One of the most effective and profitable types of material that Amos depended upon were forty-five gallon metal drums, which he used to cut open and then flatten to use as walls or roofs. With these, together with plastics and straightened wooden boxes Amos had built for himself six rooms, three of which he rented out for thirty rands per room per month. In addition he acquired a caravan through means that he did not make clear in our conversations.

The more overt appearances of these shacks encouraged more people in search of safe living space, into the area. The polarised and troubled African townships lured thousands of people away from them and into informal settlements. As the area in which Amos stayed grew in size, its residents decided, in view of the relative peace they enjoyed there, to give it a Biblical name *viz.* Canaan (the Promised Land). However the province's Ministry of Transport, which owned the land, did not take too kindly to this. After failing to evict the occupants on the grounds that it was dangerous to live there because of the unstable eca-shale[1], they numbered every shack up to 329. No more shacks were to be built thereafter in the area. A further condition was that each shack was to have only one entrance and one window. This condition was abided by up to the end of 1993. By early 1994 these conditions were totally ignored. Canaan grew in size in leaps and bounds, as did other neighbouring informal settlements. Since then, it was no mean task to estimate the number of shacks or the population in the settlement during fieldwork in later years.

Informal settlements in South Africa are an endemic feature of our history. In Clare Estate the phenomenon has conjured up various images of South Africa's past and present realities. The poverty that apartheid had engendered in the rural areas and African townships are currently manifesting itself in all the social problems that impoverishment carries with it. For many the informal settlements are the sources of the social problems that prevail in the area. There are innumerable visual illustrations of the measures that residents have taken to protect themselves from the problems that emerged since the rapid expansion of the informal settlements. In an area that once enjoyed peace and quiet, and where residents boasted of sleeping throughout the summer nights with opened windows, the situation has changed to a radically different one. Viewed from motor car windows while driving, or walking through the area, there are striking security features that now characterise the homes in Clare Estate.

To escape car-jacking many are electrifying their gates with remote control features. On the tops of fences, sharp spikes or barbed wire are attached in order to discourage burglars from climbing over them. Both gates and fences are being increasingly heightened as further deterrents to potential burglars. In the windows, balconies and verandas of many homes with custom made wrought iron burglar guards, which are firmly driven into the walls, have become standard features of security. Rottweillers, German Shepherds, American Pitbulls, Ridgebacks and other fearsome dogs patrol their masters' yards in generally aggressive style. Most were professionally trained as killer dogs and used mainly for this purpose rather than as pets. Sensor lights, which go on at the vibration of human movements, are installed in strategic places around many homes. The globes, which are a minimum of one hundred and fifty watts, are intended to surprise burglars. They cast their light very brightly and have a radius of at least twenty metres. Hi-tech security systems that are monitored by security companies and police stations are installed in almost every home. The activation of these alarms are picked up by either the monitoring security company or the local police stations, which in turn respond by sending rapid reaction units to the signalling addresses. Gun ownership and increased applications for gun licences constitute an almost full circle of security measures that Clare Estate's residents have taken to protect themselves.

Against the background of these realities, especially the fact that the established residents are of one ethnic extraction and the squatters are of another, some serious issues pertaining to ethnicity emerge. Before taking this issue any further it would be interesting to recall some of the earlier responses since 1991 to the burgeoning informal settlements in the area.

Some Early Responses

Since the beginning of 1991 residents in Clare Estate had become increasingly aware that the area was being rapidly infiltrated by African squatters from various parts of the country, but especially from within its own province of Kwa-Zulu Natal. Although there was a widespread belief that people living in the informal settlements were from the impoverished rural areas, information from the surveys done in 1991 pointed to a different scenario. Most residents were victims of the internecine violence that was taking place in the Greater Durban African townships and semi-urban areas. The violence was political and was mainly between supporters of the African National Congress and the Inkatha Freedom Party. While this was being widely covered in the media as Black on Black violence, the residents of Clare Estate, like, the residents of most other middle and upper class areas inhabited by Whites, Coloureds and Indians in other parts of South Africa, were unable to conceptualise the processes, history, events and contemporary circumstances that led to the expansion of informal settlements. The separation of residential areas by racial legislation precluded a proper understanding of these issues. It rendered most residents incapable of comprehending the extent of the violence in the townships and semi-urban areas, as well as the impact it had on their lives, social fabric and community structures.

Although, at the end of 1990 most respondents recognised the potential threats posed by the informal settlements, they remained indifferent to them for two reasons. First, many believed that complaints to the local authorities *i.e.* the Durban City Council, about the situation would be ineffective. Its all White members had a reputation for not giving sympathetic consideration to problems in Indian Group Areas. Some respondents dwelt on a conspiracy theory believing that White officials were encouraging Africans to squat in Indian Group Areas in order to induce racial friction. And second, others believed that the situation was confinable and did not expect the settlements to proliferate as they already have. By early 1992 the social problems that are usually associated with impoverishment and relative affluence began to emerge.

For many of the Indian residents Canaan was an untapped market that was waiting to be harnessed by the advantages of their capitals and better knowledge of accessibility to consumer goods at lower prices. Along the fences and pavements of one of the main arteries of Clare Estate *viz*., Clare Road, and from the garages of many homes, residents began setting up petty commodity stalls to attract the business of Canaan's residents. Basic vegetables such as onions, potatoes, tomatoes and cabbages were displayed on makeshift stalls. When the sale of these products was seen to be producing rewarding returns the range of services steadily increased. Those who had the advantage of space through their garages began retailing refrigerated cold drinks, cigarettes, canned beans and fish, frozen poultry, offal, paraffin, mealie meal, mealie rice, samp, wood and charcoal for fuel, and even water. Two major corner stores, owned by Indians in Clare Road, had drastically reoriented their businesses to meet the needs of the growing African clientele. Apart from capturing the major share of the business in the items mentioned above, these stores also capitalised on the lack of water supply in Canaan. Shopkeepers soon became the major retailers of water to the informal residents at fifty cents per twenty-five litres.

Water in the area became a highly politicised issue. The Durban City Council (D.C.C.) initially refused to situate taps at strategic points in Canaan because they believed that its residents would see this as an endorsement of their illegal occupation of unsuitable and unstable land. Canaan's residents, in their early stages sought water from nearby flowing streams and from a tap granted by the Durban City Council to another neighbouring informal settlement. This settlement was a minimum ten minutes walk away from Canaan and was separated by a six lane national highway *i.e.* the N2, a hill of approximately three kilometres in length upon which many houses were built, and a road that services this residential area. Informal residents here objected to Canaan's residents use of their tap because it lengthened their queues for water. There were additional accusations that Canaan's residents' did not treat the service with the respect it deserved. Canaan's residents' accessibility to the tap became questionable and on at least two occasions differences flared up into violent clashes. In addition, Canaan's residents return journey with the water was an even longer, more arduous one. With their twenty-five litre containers of water strenuously swaying on their heads, many have fallen victim to the perennially speeding traffic on the N2 road—some of whom were killed instantly.

When their neighbouring informal residents eventually forbade Canaan's residents from using their tap, pressure on the front yard taps of Clare Road's residents increased significantly. By February 1992 the D.C.C. admitted the difficulties and political implications of ignoring the plight of Canaan, especially since the unbanning of the extra-parliamentary movements the year before. As an admission of their difficulty to relocate Canaan's residents to more suitable conditions, one tap was at long last situated on its eastern entrance. It served more than three thousand people. The requirement was that the residents pay a monthly fee of two rands per household. This collection system was unsuccessful and people were then asked to pay for water as they came for it at twenty cents per twenty-five litres.

By July 1993 a committee member estimated the population of Canaan to be in the region of fifteen thousand people. Hence the need for more taps became obvious. By October 1993 a second tap was granted on the south-western corner of Canaan. The newly introduced payment system of "pay as you take" did not last long either. More politicised residents, having recognised the strength of their numbers and the difficulties the D.C.C. would have in withdrawing the service of the water supply, tried to mobilise residents against paying for water. When their attempts failed a frustrated activist shot and killed the person responsible for recording and collecting money for water. The service in this tap was immediately discontinued by the D.C.C. for at least one month.

Once again residents of the informal settlement were in desperate need of water. While many purchased water from the local shops and residents, others found other ways of acquiring it. One devious method that became common was to fill their containers late at night and after midnight when residents were asleep. Clare Estate's residents began protesting about receiving incessantly high water bills. Numerous media reports revealed that water bills increased by up to five hundred per cent and more in one month. While the D.C.C. initially responded insensitively to these queries about inflated water bills, many residents were threatened with their lives or were warned that informal residents would burn down their houses if they were stopped from filling water. Virtually every household thereafter removed their outside taps.

The process of removing taps planted the seeds of a newly found consciousness and solidarity among the residents in Clare Estate. This factor, together with the increasing crime in the area gave rise to the mobilisation of residents who once had a reputation for being indifferent towards their own civic problems. Many civic organisations such as the Clare Estate Ratepayers Association and resident religious bodies rallied to either assist or protest against the presence of informal settlements in the area. The local South African Police Stations acted upon a mandate to create structures that attempted to foster better understanding and relations between the established residents and informal settlements. These efforts enjoyed only limited success.

Individual Perceptions and Organised Responses

In most interviews concerning the presence of squatters in Clare Estate, it was difficult to ascertain consistent responses from them. Conversations usually began with some form of racist remark about Africans, or with gestures such as throwing of hands into the air and expressing disgust at the situation. It was clear however, whether the residents were in sympathy with the squatters or against them, that there was unanimity in the view that they should be removed.

Those who showed sympathy with them were in the minority. They were mainly from the educated elite who had an understanding of the events that led to the formation of informal settlements. Some did attempt, on an *ad hoc* basis, to play a conciliatory role between the residents and informal settlements. They tried to nurture an understanding of the divisive history of White domination of South Africa in order to explain the contemporary circumstances. This was done on public platforms, at family and social gatherings, and in one to one conversations. The aim of these individuals was constructive and conciliatory. Their intention was to contribute, in their own small ways, to breaking down the historically entrenched racial barriers that were consolidated under apartheid between Indians and Africans. One important aspect in their mission was to foster a sense of mutual appreciation of one another and acceptance of the different social and cultural backgrounds.

Other individuals from among the sympathetic ones went further in taking this mission forward. They either became pioneers in community based projects or they attached themselves to existing civic organisations in order to address the issue of informal settlements. These individuals were playing an instrumental role in keeping the peace between the established residents and those of Canaan, as well as of other informal settlements. The Clare Estate Ratepayers Association was one such platform from which they worked—an organisation that was in existence for several decades. In the absence of state initiatives to foster inter-cultural understanding to break down social barriers, it was such civic organisations that introduced a more liberal perspective on the informal settlements. In several instances they negotiated with:

1. Religious bodies to mobilise the neighbouring communities to provide health care, food and clothing.
2. The D.C.C. to provide water, and advise on sanitation services, as well as advice on alternative locations for informal settlements.
3. The South African Police to adopt a more sensitive and sympathetic approach towards Canaan.
4. Numerous sectors of the community to establish liaison committees in order to build up the trust and sensitivity in an environment that desperately needed it.

Their efforts were significantly rewarding in that they succeeded in getting the co-operation of all major role players in Clare Estate and even beyond, but only to a lesser extent with the residents who saw themselves as victims.

One such illustration of this is the Police-Public Relations Forum that was inspired by these well meaning community members and initiated by two members of the South African Police. In July 1993 both members identified at least forty-eight informal settlements within the radius of the areas they patrolled *viz.* Asherville, Springfield, Reservoir Hills, Sydhenam, Overport, Sherwood and Clare Estate. They invited all chairpersons and other senior committee members in informal settlement structures to a meeting with themselves and community representatives. Their aim was to engender trust and good relationships between the established residents and themselves. The meeting was a success and there was agreement that it should continue on a monthly basis. By the end of 1994 several senior officers in the South African Police expressed their satisfaction with this unofficial initiative and asked for the structure to be formalised. This offer motivated other such initiatives in the Greater Durban Area, which eventually led to the formation of a regional liaison body. One of the major successes of this initiative was the relatively easy entry of police into the informal settlements for routine patrols and investigations, and the co-operation of informal residents in the identification of criminals. The police claimed that their investigations in informal settlements was made easier since their public relations initiative. A number of cases were more easily solved because of it and this helped to control the escalation of crime in Clare Estate.

However, many residents remained unconvinced about this view. They believed that the crime was uncontrollable and was likely to remain that way for as long as the informal settlements remained in their suburbs. One mature response about the Clare Estate situation was once made in a convincing tone. The words were: "*You cannot have peaceful co-existence between two racial groups that mistrusted each other ever since they came into contact. One group feels more brutalised and impoverished than the other does and they stake their claim to the areas they occupy on the basis of their Africaness. The other group on the other hand,* i.e. *'We Indians' have worked very hard for what we have. Yet Africans believe that we took all this from them. They outnumber us, so how can we win*". This statement was made by one of those residents did not share the perceptions, vision and positions of his liberal counterparts. He belonged to the majority group who made up the disappointed, disillusioned and conservative elements of Clare Estate. In personal conversations and in public meetings they expressed their total outrage at the existence of informal settlements in the area. The extent of the crimes, especially in daylight robberies when women are alone at home, armed hold-ups in homes in any part of the day or night, theft of drying clothes from washing lines, carjackings and car break-ins, stealing of children's toys from the yards when they are unattended, assaults, murders and rapes became unbearable problems to them. In addition the sight of the structures in Canaan was considered as an unwanted intrusion to the aesthetic surroundings of the area.

Like their liberal counterparts, the conservative individuals had also found that the organisations that tended to their civic issues and informal settlements, served as convenient arenas to mobilise support for their views as well. In each of the monthly meetings of the executive of the Clare Estate Ratepayers Association as well as the several public meetings they held, the antagonism against the informal settlements dominated the meetings. Apart from the popular outcry against crimes in the area, two other related areas of concern emerged. First, was the rapid deterioration in the quality of life in Clare Estate and the possible breakdown of civil order. Interviewees frequently referred to the drastic slowing down of the school syllabus as an indication of this. This, several teachers claimed, had become necessary since the intake of large numbers of African pupils—who needed greater familiarisation with the English language—the medium of instruction. The closing down of several shops which had fallen victim to several attacks in a short space of time made their purchases of incidental needs problematic in that they felt too unsafe to send their children to shops that were then further away from their homes. The need to safeguard themselves against the prevailing insecurity gave rise to expensive security measures. The effect of this has been evacuation of homes by a number of residents who fled the suburb out of sheer fear and frustration. This had a drastic impact in their normal social life, which was characterised by evening and weekend visits to the area by family and friends. Frequent thefts of radios and other items from vehicles had significantly reduced the frequency with which family and friends visited one another for fear of falling victim to such criminal activities. A number of respondents complained that family members had stopped visiting them in the evenings and weekends because they felt insecure with the squatters in the area. The topography and relatively small plots of the property owners often compelled visitors to park on the pavements instead of parking inside the yards of their hosts, thereby increasing their exposure to the criminal elements. This led to a hardening of attitudes towards African squatters by the residents.[2]

These circumstances also led to the rapid devaluation of land and houses—which many tried to sell but failed because of the informal settlements. Others have tried to use their houses as collateral for loans to finance extensions to their houses or for business interests elsewhere, but were either refused loans or had their assets drastically reduced in valuation because Clare Estate was declared by the lending institutions as a high-risk area.

These factors have for the first time in more than forty years created a level of solidarity that has helped to mobilise the residents of Clare Estate to collectively fight for the official recognition of their plight. They are currently using this situation to wage a war against another aspect of the past *viz*. the taxation system of their properties. Since the 1960s residents demonstrated how apartheid structures in local authorities such as the D.C.C. have engaged in a conspiracy to falsely inflate the value of land and houses in Indian dominated Group Areas. The aim was to give higher ratings to properties in order to eke out higher yearly taxation on them. White dominated areas paid fifty per cent and less than these amounts in land and house taxes. African residential areas on the other hand did not pay rates on houses and land. In every executive and public meeting of the Clare Estate Ratepayers Association (C.E.R.A.), the problems of inflated rates and taxes, and of the informal settlements took priority.

In two of the three C.E.R.A. public meetings I attended there was an almost all Indian audience of about four hundred. The moods of these meetings were vociferously against two things. First, there were continuous attacks against the D.C.C. for remaining a white dominated structure, even after the repeal of apartheid and the general election in April 1994. There was unanimous support for the cries against racism and the unfair system of rates and taxes in Indian areas. Similar responses were received when individuals took the platform to accuse White officials of engaging in a conspiracy to tolerate informal settlements in Indian dominated areas in order to subtly induce racial friction between Indians and Africans, and so spare themselves of the accusations of racism and mismanagement. Second, there was a majority sentiment that the informal settlements be immediately relocated, and that the local authorities take responsibility for this.

The third meeting was in November 1995 and was interestingly different. For the first time a number of committee members from

Canaan and surrounding informal settlements, and a White person, attended. All were members of the African National Congress and were nominees on the recently instituted local authority *viz.* Transitional Metropolitan Council (T.M.C.). Several of these individuals took the floor after the chairperson delivered his twenty minute introductory address. They spoke in very conciliatory terms and appealed to the residents for patience and understanding of their circumstances. One squatter settlement's committee member captured the attention of the crowd when he declared total support for the residents fight against crime and the removal of Canaan and other settlements from Clare Estate. He made a passionate plea for all to remain patient until suitable alternative locations and accommodation were found for them. Another female member of his team then spoke as a representative of all Clare Estate on the T.M.C. She had to quickly retract this tone when she was challenged by a member in the meeting about the legitimacy of such a claim. A third informal settlement member appealed to the house not to racialise the discourse about the rates and squatter settlement issues. The residents who challenged him by accusing informal residents of targeting Indian areas only to settle too quickly rebuffed him. Whites, they claimed were intolerant of such formations and would rid their areas immediately if they attempted to create settlements near their suburbs. One frustrated resident challenged, to a loud applause, the White member of the A.N.C./T.M.C. in these words: *"Could the White gentleman from the T.M.C. please give us Indians the solution to keep these African squatters out of our areas. Who is he to tell us to bear this situation when they are living comfortably in their areas? I am totally fed up with these squatters because I have lost more than thirty thousand rands worth of tools. These are the people who have stolen them. And every one of my neighbours has been hit. We are living in total frustration and fear"*. The White member, with clam understanding and patience, responded to this emotional outburst: *"I appeal to you once again to co-operate with us so that we may relocate these unfortunate people in an orderly way"*.

While the T.M.C. members sounded persuasive and convincing some residents did not hesitate to bring to the house's attention that their presence was linked to the postponed local authority elections in Kwa-Zulu Natal that were rescheduled for March 1996. There was caution expressed about the persuasive talk of political parties when they are out campaigning for votes. Despite the differences of opinion and sometimes heated and emotional debates, the meeting ended amicably with consensus resolutions for further liaisons among the different groups and for further negotiations with the D.C.C.

Conclusion

The issues discussed in this chapter are intended to highlight an aspect which research on informal settlements in South Africa has ignored. The circumstances that lead to people living in informal settlements, their squalid conditions, and environmental impact are usually the targets of journalistic or investigative research. While these are crucial issues in research for various purposes we must not ignore the devastating impact it has on those who are part of a long generation of people who contributed towards the areas infrastructural development. In the number of papers that McCarthy and Hindson (1994) edited and presented in their book, not a single paper dealt with the impact that the informal settlements have had on the established residents in Durban. For this reason it is unlikely that it will have a productive impact on policy formulation. When academics of their calibre do research on such a topic, guide and edit others work, and qualify for large amounts of funding, as they did for this exercise, their work should focus on influencing policy making on a broad front. The entire book is extracted out of survey type material that discusses issues in very generalised terms. In addition its title "They Are Here To Stay..." suggests a permanency about informal settlements in South Africa's urban areas, and a sense of helplessness of our society to act upon this problem innovatively. Their recommendation is to upgrade informal settlements in most of South Africa's urban areas.

Their position has resonance with the guidelines of the ANC's Reconstruction and Development Programme (now abandoned) for the country—the aim of which is to rapidly urbanise South Africa's African population. It appears to be guided by the beliefs that this will be the surest way of social service delivery to the most downtrodden segment of its population, as well as social integration of the various ethnic and racial groups. Researchers such as Hindson and McCarthy (1994) as well as the politicians remain adamant about this. I contend here that in view of some of the issues this chapter raises, the above position is dangerously incorrect. Recent history has demonstrated to us that no post-colonial or developing state has successfully integrated its impoverished masses into its structures. Where people have moved in droves to metropolitan centres elsewhere in Africa, or in Asia or Latin

America, experience has taught us that informal settlements provide more problems than solutions. In South Africa, as much as they have been necessary places of relief for those affected by township violence and rural poverty, informal settlements should not be "...here to stay". Their impact has been seen in the disruptive anti-social behaviour it has generated by the armed robberies, assaults, rapes, murders and other thefts in the affected areas. The rapid devaluation of land and houses, and the rapid deterioration of the environments within informal settlements, had broken the morale of the residents and exacerbated the brain drain in South Africa. The poverty, created by virtue of high density living and a lack of space to grow crops in the squatter camps has also produced an extremely large number of beggars who move from house to house and who beg at traffic lights. The insecurity has made the residents prone to conspiracy theories about beggars. Many are often of the belief that thieves first tend to visit their homes under the guise of begging, but are in actual fact surveying the place to provide information to others or to rob them at a later date. The broader impact of this situation is that it has impacted negatively on other forms of infrastructural development such as tourism and has rapidly slowed down the pace of work in schools after taking in large numbers of children from the squatter camps. Overall, the pressure that the squatter camps have exerted on public services such as health care, water supply, ecosystems and education, has been extremely costly and has exacerbated racial tension between Africans and Indians.

Together, these issues point towards the enormous difficulties that the metropolitan centres in South Africa will be facing in this challenging period of transformation and reconstruction. A demotivated middle class, such as Indian homeowners in Clare Estate, could sink into a state of economic apathy or simply emigrate. This could do irreparable damage to the infrastructure of the region, as it had done in countries like Uganda, Tanzania and Kenya. It is because the labour, knowledge and taxes of highly motivated and hard-working middle classes, more than that of the upper and under classes, that sustains the economies in any situation. South African policy makers should take a leaf out of the present development process of one of the very few African countries that is showing genuine signs of progress. The country is Ghana. A recent CNN documentary has shown that General Rawlings's Policy of reduced reliance on foreign investment and International Monetary Fund Loans, and of redistributing major resources for rural development, has created sufficient incentive for

Ghanaians to return to the rural areas to rebuild their lives. The idea should not be to create unnecessarily high expectations with South Africa's impoverished masses. Instead, it should be to educate them realistically on what the resources of the country can afford to deliver and by when in their lives they should be able to reap the benefits of their sweat and toil. It is not unlikely, they should be told that they might only conveniently acquire the comforts of the latest technologies two or three generations hence. As one visiting retired United Nations seed geneticist and agricultural development advisor from Trinidad-Tobago suggested in a visit to Durban: *"South Africa need to teach their poor how to live, instead of keeping them waiting for houses they may never be able to pay for, or for jobs they are unlikely get in an environment that looks for the cheapest way out in everything they produce"*. If South African policy makers can take such advise seriously enough, they would be contributing more positively to the negativity that has engulfed Clare Estate and other affected areas.

REFERENCES

1. Very unstable sedimentary rock formations having the property of splitting into thin layers. Building on such ground requires specially engineered foundations.
2. By June 1999, after the research for this project was completed, residents began expressing feelings of relief that the settlement had been almost totally dismantled and that this augured well for a return to normal lifestyle.

CHAPTER FOUR

Small Business Opportunities and Informal Settlements

Introduction

The rapid increase in the population sizes in the squatter camps radically altered the dynamics of movements and requirements of the residents who shared the living spaces in the research areas. There were as a result of this, two segments within the areas *i.e.* the established tax paying residents and the squatters who acquired a degree of legitimacy that included representation in the Durban City Council, as well as voting rights for local councillors. Their legal status encouraged many to expand upon their dwelling sizes and increase the number who shared the spaces under a single roof. This added to the number of people who began building new structures in the squatter camps, who in turn brought in more people. As a result emerging characteristic features in the squatter camps were high density of people and high unemployment.

The visibility of the unemployed people was obvious in several ways. During the day most either spent time outside their dwellings in view of passing motorists and the residents, or walked up and down the streets either aimlessly or looking for casual work with the residents. In several daytime visits to the outer rings of the squatter camps there were groups of young men seen gambling with cards, drinking beer and cooking food. Others simply sat around talking to one another and not engaging in any activity. While some opened tuck-shops within the squatter camps, they were neither adequately stocked nor had the range of goods to meet most of the squatters requirements. Capital was the most constricting factor in the expansion of their operations. Their lack of privately owned transport, a lack of knowledge to purchase in ways and places that saved on their buying and that could increase their profits, and the refusal of wholesaling companies to deliver in the squatter camps added to their difficulties as nascent entrepreneurs.

These features within the squatter camps added a new dimension to the character of the research areas. As populations whose marginalised statuses did not allow them to travel freely, the squatters provided a captive market for many Indian residents. They were better endowed than the squatters by virtue of their surplus capital and privately owned transport that encouraged many to engage in casual to more formalised types of retail trading. The latter type of traders should not be confused as retailers who operate in licensed, fully equipped shops that are sanctioned by the laws and bye-laws of the Durban Municipality. Their formalised trading actually constituted an operation from an enclosed space such as a garage or a part of the house, both of which were road facing and which were transformed for purposes of trading.

Trading in Context

Understanding the relative successes of smaller unlicenced traders (hereafter referred to as traders), who operated either from the pavements or from part of their houses, require an understanding of how licenced businesses have been affected since transformation. Since 1994 the number of armed robberies that took place in businesses escalated at alarming levels. Shopkeepers reacted by opening later in the mornings when the streets became busier, ensured that there was always more than one person in the shop at any one time and that they were armed with guns, closing early in the evenings when it was safer to do so, and either selling their shops or just disengaging from business altogether because of their failure to sell their shops or to operate profitably. Of all the shopkeepers who were interviewed, everyone of them had related an unpleasant experience with robbers either in their shops or at their homes. Since all have been family operated businesses, family members became inevitable victims. The casualties ranged from being traumatized to being stabbed or shot to death. The case studies below are constructed from interviews with shopkeepers who operated within a radius of just a kilometre from each other.

> Mr. M., a shopkeeper for more than forty years, inherited his general dealer business from his late father in 1969. It was then situated in a different location about a kilometre away from where

he was operating at the time of the interview. He worked with two other brothers who, like him, were married with children and living in their own houses. The profit from the business was shared equally among all three brothers. They considered it a thriving business and lived comfortably after paying all their monthly debts and overheads. Between 1994 and June 1997 they were held up three times in their shop and twice at home. On one occasion one of the brothers was severely beaten with the butt of a gun, while in another occasion at home the interviewee, his wife, mother and a sister who was visiting during the day, were badly beaten and robbed. His wife spent two weeks in hospital with a swollen face, injured ribs and severe trauma. His confidence in the business fell drastically after June 1997 because of these incidents. From January 1997 he installed wrought iron gates and served their customers from behind them. However, the volume of his business took a serious downward turn when a neighbour, two doors away, first started selling fruit and vegetables from his garage. As the new neighbouring enterprise improved the competitor increased his range of stock in groceries, directly affecting the former's family business. In August 1997 Mr. M and his brothers decided to sell the lease of their business, but were forced to abandon it after failing to find a buyer.

Mrs. M.E. rented a shop directly opposite a squatter camp named Lusaka, about one kilometre away from Mr. M. above. Robbers shot dead the previous owner of the shop in 1995. This discouraged others from taking over the premises for at least eight months, until Mrs. M.E. and her husband decided to take the risk of running it at a significantly reduced rental. Since then they were robbed three times, in April 1996, August 1997 and March 1999 respectively. She ran the shop with her husband and was helped by her unemployed nephew at least three days a week. In April 1996 her husband was robbed when he was alone, but was not physically harmed. In August 1997 her nephew was held up and shot in the stomach. Fortunately he recovered in hospital and was back at work after three months. Allegedly there were women across the road that witnessed the incident but were too afraid to give evidence to the police. Two arrests were made for the shooting but the suspects were released because nobody was willing to give evidence against them. In March 1999 Mrs. M.E., her husband

> and nephew, were accosted once again by two robbers. This time however, Mrs. M.E.'s husband was better prepared and had already suspected the two from the time he opened his shop. He cocked his gun and had it ready. At first one went into the shop and bought a box of matches, and later the other came for the same thing. The third time they walked into the shop together. Mr. M.E. asked his nephew to serve them, while he stood with the gun in his hands. As he suspected, one of the two robbers produced a homemade gun and pointed it to his nephew while the other raised his hand with a long knife warning them to cooperate. Mr. M.E. unhesitatingly, but surprisingly, raised his hands and shot both of them, killing one and seriously wounding the other. With both in their fifties, and two of their children still studying, Mr. and Mrs. M.E. found it difficult to close down the business and do something else. They considered themselves too old to divert their energies in another enterprise, despite their meagre earnings and high risks in a volatile area. They had one of two places to go to *i.e.* Cape Town where her brother lived, or overseas, "anywhere there's peace and respect for life". In October 1999 they abandoned the shop.

As a result of incidents fear and paranoia among business people reached obsessive levels. Several interviewees have as a result started trading behind wrought iron gates to keep clients outside the shop and reduce their chances of being robbed.

Opening and closing shops later and early respectively, and disengagement from business created opportunities for the potential unlicenced traders. Many Indians took the risk of by setting up stalls on the pavements, but withdrew from such a practice within a short period because all of them had become victims of thieves. The stall operators were from both gender groups and from a range of age groups and employment backgrounds. Early morning trade proved to be lucrative. They opened earlier than the normal shops in order to serve pedestrians on their way to work, from the squatter camps. There was a simple logic to this—most did not have the firewood to prepare meals early morning—so bread, eggs, tinned fish or beans were ideal items to sell to them for their lunches. The early morning human traffic became a thriving market for many of these traders—who enjoyed eventually enjoyed the confidence of the major bread suppliers and other wholesalers who delivered to their doors—after so many of the formal businesses closed down and the suppliers aversion to deliver to small enterprises in the squatter camps. The manufacturers and wholesalers recognised the potential market in the squatter camps and agreed to deliver to the household enterprises, despite the protest from licensed shopkeepers. The latter complained about the rapid decline in their businesses because of the proliferation of unlicensed traders. However, these stalls provided conveniences for the working people and others from the squatter camps because of their proximity to them. Unlike the stalls and tuck shops within the squatter camps, the household run stalls had a wider range of goods at generally more competitive prices. The one item that the squatters could not avoid from the household stalls was bread. This requirement induced other purchases such as tinned food, paraffin, frozen chicken, maize meal, candles, firewood and other basic incidental items.

The experiences of hold-ups led the traders as well to work with the same caution and security of the licensed shopkeepers. They too started trading with anxiety and from behind wrought iron bars—their working patterns showing signs that are symptomatic of the unfolding violence in post-apartheid South Africa.

An Insight into the Unlicensed Traders Operations

Most, if not all household members were engaged either full time or peripherally in the trading activities. These household enterprises expanded to a point that required inputs from more than one person, as well as space that could adequately cater for the things they knew were profitable and quick to retail. The enormity of the tasks eventually gave way to a distinct gender and aged based division of labour. Work for most traders began from about 04h00 in the summer months and 05h00 in the winter months, and ended not earlier than 20h00. The day usually began with women's domestic duties in their kitchens, when they saw to the needs of their school-going children, their working husbands and other household members, and later to the general neatness of the home. The business activities usually began around 5h30 to service the early morning commuters going to work. Among those who retailed fruit and vegetables work had to begin before this time for at least three days of the week. This was determined by the working hours of what is generally referred to as "the bulk market" in Central Durban, where wholesalers in fruit and vegetables sell in bulk to retailers for resale to the public. The operating hours of the bulk market are from 04h00 in the mornings and at most times require that business people do their purchasing early in the mornings from this hour to ensure that they get quality goods. On these days work actually begins for the women of the household from around 03h00 to provide breakfasts for those who do the marketing. The efficiency with which the traders do their work demonstrates a range of factors relating to the successes in their enterprises. Many have had to work with brute determination to survive because they were victims of unemployment that was brought about through retrenchments, resignations from work out of frustration with their working conditions, or through a shortage of work in their particular fields. Others among the traders included pensioners and housewives. In most of these enterprises they were also helped by school-going children and others who were in tertiary institutions, as well as by friends and relatives who helped only to keep busy during the day, without any remuneration.

The details of the daily lives of twelve unlicensed operators were collected through regular visits between February and November 1998. Some basic information is illustrated in Table 4.1 followed by information about how some of these traders had to reshape their working lives.

Table 4.1: Illustrating number (1) household size (2), number in formal employment (3), previous employment of stall holders (4), range of goods (5), type of clientele (6), and number of working hours per day (7) (The number in brackets indicates the issues in the table below)

1	*2*	*3*	*4*	*5*	*6*	*7*
1	6	0	Building trade; heavy duty driver	Firewood, candles, paraffin, vegetables	Mainly squatters	12
2	2	0	Plasterer/tiler	Groceries	Mainly squatters	16
3	5	0	Shop assistant	Groceries, firewood	Mainly squatters	16
4	5	0	Vegetable stall in Durban market	Groceries, fruit, vegetables, frozen chicken	Mixed	16
6	7	1	Taylor in a clothing factory	Regular Beer, liquor, African beer	Mainly Africans	18
7	6	0	Shebeen	African beer, regular beer, liquor	Mainly Indians	10
8	6	2	Vegetable stall in Durban market	Vegetables, fruit, poultry	Mainly Indians	12
9	7	1	Bricklayer	Vegetables, fruit	Mixed	8
10	4	1	Market gardener	Vegetables, fruit	Mainly squatters	10
11	13	0	Vegetable stall in the market	Vegetables, poultry	Mainly Indians	12
12	8	2	Builder	Vegetables	Mainly squatters	10

A number of interesting factors emerge from Table 4.1. Only five of the twelve households had people who were engaged in wage or salaried employment. In three of these five cases (numbers 8, 9 and 12) the working members' salaries were crucial to the survival of the household. The profits from their trading did not yield sufficient returns to meet their expenses, but only meagrely complemented the wages and salaries that were brought into the household. All three were property owners. In these cases it was the retired first generations from within the households who engaged in fruit and vegetable retailing. Their responses to questions about the reasons for their trade were unanimous about the difficulties of meeting basic expenses—especially paying their property taxes. Each of the traders operated from makeshift mobile stalls that were set up every morning and dismantled every evening. Their range of mainly vegetables and to a lesser extent fruit evidently made them significantly smaller traders than the other nine mentioned in the table.

It is apparent from Table 4.1 that all of the traders' previous employment was not in professional fields—placing them in terms of their resources in the lower middle class category. They were residents in their respective areas for four decades and more. Those who worked in the building trade were either retired or frustrated in trying to acquire secure employment. One of the respondents stated that Indian tradesmen were being ousted from the industry by cheaper African labour. This point was evident in the contemporary building construction industry in Durban—in recession from the early 1980s. Africans were previously excluded from engaging in skilled labour, so their entry into the building industry brought them in at significantly lower rates than qualified and certified Indian tradesmen. The building industry in South Africa also suffered a major recession in the late 1970s and did not recover since then. It marginalised a number of its employees and forced them to seek alternative sources of income. Others who have either been market gardeners or stall owners in the Central Durban market have had various experiences that also had a racial basis to it. The market gardener reflected in the table lost his farm in 1968 in the Springfield Flats area when it was expropriated through the 1950 Group Areas Act. This forced him to relocate to the market where he had to shift from being a producer and wholesaler of vegetables to one who had to start buying to sell as a retailer. But like the other market stall owners he had to leave the market because it was being over traded by African "squatter sellers"—who entered the market in large numbers and sold from the pavements outside the market and from empty spaces inside the market. The Durban City Council, the official administrators, alleged that it was unable to control the "squatter sellers" because of their sheer numbers and the risk of being accused for acting with racial bias against Africans.

Those who made a living out of shebeens were from two different backgrounds. One became unemployed after the men's suit factory (number 6) in which he worked drastically retrenched staff in 1994, while the other (number 7) ran his shebeen independently for at least thirty years. The difference in these operations was that the items they sold were not publicly displayed like those of their fruit and vegetable counterparts. During apartheid, such businesses were under constant surveillance by the police because they were not tolerated. Since the early 1990s, laws against shebeens were relaxed, but they had to acquire official approval from the local authorities. The two individuals engaged in the same trade for different reasons and were affected in different ways after the 1994 election. While one operated with relative ease over the last thirty years the other functioned under constant threat of being reported by his neighbours and raids by police.

> K.P., an unmarried 57 years old man, was seriously injured in a fight in 1968. After his recovery he was considered unemployable because his right hand was disabled. In 1969, in the absence of close enough bar, he decided to capture the market by opening a shebeen—especially since his friends were regular drinkers and there was no place for them to socialise in the evenings and weekends. He knew he could draw their attention towards his enterprise at home, which was separated from the rest of his family's privacy. Up to 1993 his clientele were mainly Indians. But after this period he spread word around in the squatter camps, through friends, that he was selling African beer. Over a period of six months his clientele changed to 40 per cent African and 60 per cent Indian. However only known Africans were allowed to sit in for their drinks. The normal service to Africans was to take away only. K.P.'s service extended to at least 18 hours a day because that is all he ever did. His business approach was only through local networking and he enjoyed the company of friends who took turns to stay overnight with him.

> S.R., a 46 years old retrenched tailor, started his shebeen in August

1995 when he decided he was too frustrated to continue looking for employment and found his savings was being drastically eroded through household expenses. Selling liquor was unthinkable at one stage and was totally against his moral values. But, he claimed, survival had urged him into doing so and that it was the quickest way to replenish his savings. His house was situated on a road that was regularly used by squatters from a neighbouring camp about one hundred metres away. Regular and African beer was especially touted with the squatters who eventually began to support him in large numbers. The City Council refused him permission to operate a shebeen, therefore making his enterprise unlicensed and illegal. He complained that the neighbours continuously objected to the sight of Africans frequenting his house to buy liquor and threatened to report him to the police. He managed to win their confidence by a careful challenge to them to find him employment, promising to stop his venture if this was done for him. He believed this generated some sympathy from his neighbours, but at a cost. He was to refrain from selling his items at night because of the fear of attracting the wrong people who were suspected of mingling with the genuine clients and who are generally suspected of crimes against them. Hence his working hours were reduced in comparison with his counterpart K.P. above.

It is apparent from Table 4.1 that the working hours of these respondents are longer than usual. The figures in the last column reveal an average of approximately thirteen hours per day, making it five hours higher than the normal working day in South Africa. The difference between the two case studies above was that one felt a sense of protection because the former was mainly patronised by old friends and known district people, while the latter had risked exposing himself to totally unknown people from a racial group widely perceived to be harbouring culprits. Hence the number of working hours between them was vastly different. Both however ensured that men did the work and served their clients. Conventional norms in Indian households forbid women from participating in these kinds of activities, although their support in these two cases was less visible.

Among the fruit and vegetable sellers there was a profound division of labor, but with more visible support from the women. The first four listed in Table 4.1 operated as two pairs of neighbours with tacit understandings of each other's businesses. Numbers 1 and 2 were immediately adjacent to each other while numbers 3 and 4 were about 40 metres apart from each other and about a kilometre away from numbers 1 and 2. Numbers 1, 2 and 3 converted their motor car garages into shops, while number 4 extended his house to create an enclosed space for his business. In the cases of numbers 1 and 2 their enterprises were intended to complement each other, especially after the shop close by closed down after its third brutal robbery, in which two people were killed and another seriously injured. The closure provided an opportunity for them, which was grasped soon after. As old friends they were supportive of each other and regularly discussed their day's activities. Their years of association and operating in close proximity to each other could be equated to a social club because it drew other district friends and nearby relatives to them at all times of the day. While one sold groceries and frozen food, the other sold domestic fuel items such as firewood, paraffin and candles. The men ran both stalls with active support in the trading only sometimes from women, as illustrated below.

> I.M., a 52 two years old unmarried plasterer, gave up looking for employment in his trade since 1992. His complaint was against the cheaper African tradesmen that building firms were hiring. Against the amount that he used to earn, he considered it too demeaning to return to the trade after cheap African labour underrated the value of his work. He started his business in March 1995, but stopped it in August after he was robbed at gunpoint. He reopened it in December 1995 but stopped it again in July 1996 after his nephew, who stayed with him, committed suicide. He restarted in November 1997, but this time with metal gates blocking the steel door and a small opening cut out from the metal gates to serve his clients. He was barely visible from the road because of this precautionary gate. He began work at 5h30 and closed between 22h00 and 23h00 everyday. He lived with a friend in his three bedroom flat that was part of a three-floor building. Below his flat were two other flats, which were occupied by his two married sisters and their families. Both helped him when he needed assistance and cooked his food by taking turns. All three households paid significantly reduced rent because the building was directly opposite a squatter camp (Canaan). Under the circumstances the occupants of the flats believed that their occupation of the building was more of a favour to the landlords than for their own benefit.

> G.H., a seventy-two years old retired plasterer decided to trade from his garage and incorporate into his activities his two unmarried unemployed sons—one a plasterer and the other a heavy duty driver. While both sons complained of the difficulties of finding work, their parents also complained of their alcoholic behaviour. The parents thought it was appropriate to trade with the squatters and hopefully keep their sons' minds occupied and away from liquor. They succeeded only up to a point in disciplining them. When business improved by selling paraffin and firewood, G.H. decided to buy a deep freeze from which he started selling frozen chicken and chicken giblets. This investment paid off well, but was stolen soon after when the garage was broken into at night and the deep freeze was taken away. He felt disinclined to continue trading and stopped for a while. When his sons returned to their drinking habits he decided to reopen. After four months from restarting, three people who made it appear as though they were from the squatter camp held up the father and two sons at gunpoint. Each of the three was badly beaten up and they all had to endure the embarrassment of not being able to defend one another. This brought an abrupt halt to their enterprise in October 1996.

While stalls 1 and 2 were operated mainly by men, the women helped by ensuring that they received their beverages, snacks and meals at the required times. Although there was a tendency to ignore the role of the women in these enterprises their contributions were equally important. The men often counted themselves only in their trading and spoke in terms of their working hours, without acknowledgement of the women. Their duties were taken for granted and not counted as substantive work that was indeed integral to the work of the men, despite the fact that they helped to clean the garages and relieve them for a few hours on the days when the men had other chores. They tended to draw a distinction between help and work.

In the cases of 3 and 4, the situations were significantly different. Both were married and had experience in retail trading. Their proximity to each other was of no consequence to their trading. While number 3 had converted his garage into a space for his retail activities, number 4 had extended his house for this purpose. Interestingly, both had licensed businesses on either side of each other, which were once thriving retail outlets. But however both closed their operations because of their inability to sustain themselves in the changing political and economic conditions. Their rentals were high and they felt that they were too easy targets for hold-ups. There was a continuous stream of pedestrian traffic for most of the day, starting from at least 05h00 and winding down after 21h00. The early morning hours and particularly the early evening hours were their busiest. Both stalls were supported by hundreds of squatters during these hours, clearly bringing in substantial amounts of cash into their businesses. The backgrounds of the men in these two outlets made them more persevering since their experience in retail empowered them in their dealings with clientele. They worked for most hours in the day and the inputs by their wives were significant and emphatically appreciated by them. But the fear under which they functioned was a perennial problem.

> A.R., a fifty years old fresh produce trader, began using his double garage early in 1992 to sell fruits and vegetables to people in his neighbourhood (emphasis on Indians). He started this business from home as an experiment to test its viability. His intention was to withdraw from trading in the market in Central Durban because "there the Africans are overcrowding us and only robbing the Indians". While he worked in the market his wife ran the business from home, producing a turnover of between R500.00-R800.00 per day. It did not take long for their efforts to show bigger returns, encouraging A.R. to entirely withdraw from his market stall. He was receiving more support than he expected because his clientele base grew substantially. From April 1994 he paid full attention to his venture from home. From August 1994 he started retailing a few grocery items such as tinned beans and fish. By October 1995 his wife was attacked and robbed. The second robbery took place in February 1996. His house was burgled twice in 1995 and 1996. After these incidents he decided to install steel burglar guards and serve clients from behind them. The house burglaries took place when nobody was inside. All four incidents occurred during the day when A.R. was absent from home. He increased his grocery selling in November 1994, directly affecting the two shops close to him. He started selling cigarettes and frozen chicken. By November 1997 he was retailing at least 1000 kilograms of chicken, 500 packets of cigarettes and at least 1000 tins of beans or fish per week, taking his daily turnover from between R500.00—R800.00 up to

R3000.00 per day. Support for his business had a distinct ethnic breakdown to it. His Indian clients supported him during the day while African clients supported him early in the morning and in the evenings. His wife usually awoke at 03h00 and he began his day from 04h00 when he had to go to the bulk market for fruits and vegetables. Thereafter she made breakfast for her two children and mother, packed her children's school lunches, cleaned her house and started trading from 06h30. A.R.'s affinity for the bulk market encouraged him to return to it, but this time as a wholesaler. He had eight stalls, which were managed by his son and younger brother. While support from the squatters had helped to finance his expansion, he felt he "...could do without African business. They have no respect for us and there is no future for us Indians in this country. I am not a racially biased person, but I worked long enough with Africans to know that they are not interested in real progress. The moment they see someone progressing they want to rob and kill him. That's why I rather take my family away to India. Over there there's lot of poverty but not so much killing and hold-ups like here!" Because of their insecurity A.R. stood outside the garage with friends while his wife traded from behind the steel burglar guards.

M.J. a 43 years old father of three children started his business in 1994. Prior to this he worked with an uncle as a shop assistant for 13 years. He later found employment with the Durban Corporation as a labourer. While he worked there he decided to emulate his neighbour A.R. and start selling fruits and vegetables to the squatters. But he had to borrow money from relatives, which he claimed he is still paying back. His day started his day at 04h00 and ended it at about 21h00. His business grew to a point of evidently turning him into a formidable competitor with his neighbour and brought about his resignation from the Durban Corporation. His space was stacked with crates of fruits and vegetables, African beer and groceries. The trading was done almost entirely by his wife while he saw to the purchasing of stock, and like A.R. he stood outside the counter area to act as a watchman for his business. M.J. had at least three burglaries that cost him an accumulated amount of R8000.00. He relied on the squatters for his survival and is unhappy to hear of their relocation through the state funded housing schemes that are being developed all over

Durban. He was optimistic about the future of the country and did not envisage emigration, despite the fact that he believed that "since the elections the country is all upside down". To him "Wherever there's people there's trouble. So where are we going to run to?" M.J. was reluctant to divulge his daily takings or the volumes that he sold per day or week. It was equally difficult to estimate how he fared with his neighbouring competitor, although he appeared confident and was happy with the success of his venture.

Both A.R. and M.J. were individuals of varying means. While the former had a relatively more convenient material background, the latter had substantially fewer comforts. But the neighbouring squatter camps provided them with opportunities to uplift their material circumstances and offset the statuses of established licensed shops. While one was able to return to the market as a wholesaler with more capital (AR), the other worked himself up to a position that permitted him to resign from a job that ensured him a regular and guaranteed income (MJ). Both their enterprises were effectively recent manifestations of post-apartheid change in Indian dominated residential areas. Their relative successes raise a number of important questions about the failure of established licensed businesses and their replacement by unlicensed smaller ventures that fall within the category of informal businesses. At least eight reasons, factual and conjecturing, could be posited as explanations for this situation. The factual situations were visible and became self-evident over time, while conjectures are based on assumptions from the ethnographic evidence:

1. The unlicensed traders operated at an advantage from the licensed shops in that their expenses were comparatively lower. The rentals and other expenses of the licensed traders were generally higher.
2. This gave the unlicensed traders the advantage of trading at lower costs, thereby drawing the bulk of the clientele towards themselves.
3. Unlike the licensed shops, their counterparts relied more on household labour than on hired labour.
4. The unlicensed traders generally came from an employment background that exposed them more to African behavioural habits and patterns of socialisation, allowing them to adapt easily to the hardy ways of people from the squatter camps.

5. Unlicensed traders appeared to gain the confidence of the squatters much faster than the shopkeepers because of this.
6. There was an apparent class distinction between the shopkeepers and the squatters, which drew a distinct line between the two groups. The latter group, as it was reported on more than one occasion, did not like the social distance that Indian business people wedged between them. They preferred a more casual approach in dealing with them—which was seriously lacking by the licensed traders. This created an aversion among the squatters to support such enterprises.
7. Through a more personlised approach towards the squatters, many of the latter were able to acquire credit that was not so easily acquired from the shopkeepers.
8. The personalised relationships allowed unlicensed traders a more informed insight into the structure and functioning of the squatter camps and their residents' requirements.

Unlicensed Traders and their Relationships with African Clientele

The relationships between African squatters and Indian traders must be understood against the background of rapid transformation that is geared towards empowering Africans, escalating violence often associated more with Africans than with the other racial categories, and the historical mutual mistrust between Africans and Indians. This is despite the general cordiality and the inter-dependence displayed between both groups. From a purely observational viewpoint, several characteristics were made obvious. The traders who did their business from behind metal and steel bars made the fear and anxiety with which they operated obvious. After their losses through theft and the violent episodes that each one suffered, they too, like the licensed shops, had to draw a line between clientele and themselves. All were fully armed with guns, always had friends and relatives with them, had monitored alarm systems, and generally operated with a constant measure of vigilance. Most unknown male clientele who were either seen for the first time or who were seen only at intervals were usually viewed with caution and suspicion. When the circumstances permitted, the practice among the traders was to quietly ask another client if the new face was a familiar one and whether he was from the neighbouring squatter camp. When no other known squatter was close, the traders either broke into their Indian dialects or gestured or whispered to one another, indicating the presence of the unknown person/s. During these moments trading was done with utmost care and a virtual readiness on the part of the male traders to fight back, run, shut the doors, or call for help. Each one had stated that their overtly demonstrated readiness had helped to foil other likely holdups on more than one occasion. The presence of neighbours at the trading outpost, the watchful eyes of the neighbours from their balconies, and their closeness to either panic buttons or the telephones were equally helpful in this regard. Another major deterrent were the signs, attached to the walls, of the security firm monitoring their alarms, with notices such as "*Armed response in under ten minutes*". Each notice had a picture of a gun and was glaring with the expectation of swift and violent responses to possible attacks. The metal and steel gates were also a wedge between traders and clients in that they helped in keeping accurate records of purchases and sales and prevented shoplifting. It was also for this reason that more than one person had to be in attendance during trading hours. While one served, the other/s kept a watchful eye on what was taken away after the exchange of money and goods. The traders reported huge losses in their stocks prior to the installation of the steel gates. After taking precautionary measures and ensuring that there was vigilant assistance at all times, they claimed that they were able to account more accurately for their stocks. For instance, ever since the gates for numbers 2, 3 and 4 were installed, and after their introduction of vigilant assistants, there were no robberies or evidence of pilfering.

But their functioning was not only about negative issues with people from the squatter camps or a one-way track of simplistic ethnic divisions. For instance, the trader's reliance on clients from the squatter camps for information on unknown faces was an indication of a developing bond among people from the two groups. Many from within the squatter camps became willingly vigilant on behalf of the traders. The squatters were aware of their hold-ups, burglaries and the generally vulnerable positions under which the traders operated. For these reasons they were genuinely empathetic and were openly supportive towards the traders. This relationship grew out of regularity of support and a growing sense of mutual respect from both sides.

The point at which the traders made their entry into the captive market in the squatter settlements was crucial for them. Those who realised that the success of their ventures depended more on the squatters than on their Indian neighbours had to be tactful. An important mechanism in this exercise was the ability to talk to the squatters in the dominant local African language *i.e.* isiZulu. This engineered an almost immediate endearing effect on the relationship between the client and service provider. Speaking in isiZulu made communication easier, facilitated an understanding of particular ethnic requirements and helped to create a congenial atmosphere to conduct business. This also proved crucial in image building with the squatters. As one trader stated: *"You got to know some of the right guys in there if you want to be safe."* A particular approach was to ensure that a close relationship was established with the executive committees in the neighbouring squatter camps. Every squatter camp had an executive committee that came into existence through a manner of voting that was actually only a semblance of democratic procedures. Most executives were "elected" in at least one of three ways *viz.*:

1. Through the popularity they achieved through their entrepreneurial skills, such as through the sale of various kinds of beer and liquor,
2. Or their oratory skills and the ability to mobilise political support for African dominated political parties, and
3. Or sheer brute strength and belonging to a powerful gang within the squatter camp.

These executives wielded significant amounts of power and enforced disciplinary codes as they saw fit—but only while they managed to last in office. Their existence enforced procedural norms that first required their recognition as the legitimate local authority. The respect they commanded encouraged the traders to befriend and consult with them on issues of common concern. Squatter executive structures were the avenues through which the traders also befriended the inhabitants within the squatter camps. This served as an effective entry point into the purchasing power within the squatter camps. Receiving the approval of the local executive was, therefore, a crucial issue in acquiring support from them. But such endeavours did not come without risks. In this type of poverty-stricken situation, where cash is not always readily available, credit and trust are two sides of the same coin. Providing credit was an important way through which the traders acquired some form of recognition and helped to concretise trust and relationship building. However credit had to be earned after the client was deemed sufficiently regular, well known to the trader and trustworthy enough to warrant it. An assessment of figures that took several months to collate because of the sensitivity of the information and the unwillingness of the traders to divulge it, revealed that at least three traders listed in Table 4.1 had amounts of R7000.00, R6500.00 and R5000.00 outstanding to them. While, from most of these amounts there was hope that the debtors will repay, a substantial amount in each case was carried over for months. Amounts of R2700.00, R2200.00 and R3500.00 were respectively carried over for a period of more than three months. These amounts, which were owed interest free, were deemed unlikely to be recovered, although the traders were still hopeful that the day might arrive when the debts could be finally settled.

There were several accounts of individuals reportedly being disciplined by the executives, after being reported by the traders. After taking the matter directly to the local executives the issues did receive their attention. The traders were satisfied that the persons responsible for the problems, especially relating to matters of bad behaviour and not paying overdue accounts, were dealt with amicably and to the satisfaction of all concerned. But the success of these cases depended upon the appropriate person being available. Many of the squatters who had debts relocated to other squatter camps or found employment in distant places and, therefore, had to relocate, making it difficult for them to trace. When relocated people were traced, the local executive did not have any jurisdiction over them and, therefore, could not enforce discipline over them. While these losses amounted to substantial figures, the traders were not constrained by them.

The social advantages in giving credit had paid off enormously in the favour of the traders. They were seen to be humane in the eyes of the squatter communities and as people who reached out to them in times of desperate need. Credit had facilitated the images of the traders in positive ways among the squatters, making them acceptable and approachable people to deal with. Their understanding of basic and incidental requirements and their provision at comparatively affordable prices were significant in the services they provided to the squatters. In addition, their proximity to the squatter camps and long hours of service that went beyond the normal trading hours, had served as centres of convenience. To some extent, the trading posts became convenient points for socialisation. Small groups were often cited standing for hours talking to each other, often drawing in the chief trader and/or his assistants into their conversations. The interactions were generally light hearted, jovial and free from any tensions and suspicions, providing situations of normalcy among familiar people. Such sights demonstrated the informality and personalised manner with which business was often conducted when familiar people were present. Many of the squatter clientele were known by their first names to the traders and their daily requirements were often given to them after gesturing or use of sign language. Often, the words "usual" were used to stipulate requirements at the point of transaction. With understanding and a willingness to serve, a parcel such as a loaf of bread, a packet of frozen chicken and a tin of beans or fish were often packed and either exchanged for the required payment or booked down as credit. These were elements of familiarity, mutual acceptance and bonding at a level that is still relatively unknown.

A Few Significant Events and Ambiguous Ethnography

Data for a number of issues required regular several visits to ensure reliability of information and its careful cross-checking. However, the nature of the responses that were collated, presented difficulties with arriving at a clear understanding of the true perceptions of most of the traders and their views on transformation. Their responses were often inconsistent and were widely determined by the pressure they felt due to the busy or difficult periods, what they felt—dependent upon what incident prevailed at a particular time, and what was being witnessed in the course of interviews and conversations. For instance, in the case of one of the respondents[1] who I visited for the third time in four weeks, a closer look at his set-up helped to acquire some familiarisation with his methods of operation and his personal views. His single garage, which was converted into a tuck shop, had well laid out shelves packed with groceries, a refrigerator, four freezers, a metal gate and a steel door, each of which had a contiguous opening of one square foot through which he served his clients. The interview began with what appeared to be a balanced perspective on the current political and social changes of what was perceived to have taken place since April 1994. His response to the issue was that there are two sides to the African majority, the government and the people who reside in the squatter camp. If one had to look at either side, he argued, then one is bound to find the good and the bad. Unfortunately, as he put it: "One bad egg among them makes everybody look bad. Not all of them (Africans) are bad." In the course of the conversation, he teased a female client, saying "Can't you and I get married now?"—acquiring a positive nod from her. At the same time he frequently referred to a seven years old African child who helped him in his business from 07h00 to 21h00, as: "You Black bastard!". The awaiting African clients, whom he evidently befriended, felt totally at ease with him and his vulgarity, and were bemused by his racially loaded jokes.

However, in one of the visits the trader's views hardened within seconds when, in the space of approximately thirty minutes, two separate fights had broken out between African youths from the neighbouring squatter camp across the road. This brought out a side of the trader that was clearly submerged. He retorted in the course of the first fight: "Ay brother, with these guys I have a very hard time. As it is on Friday night they were pulling out people's wives from their shacks and stripping them naked. The crime is gone fuckin' high here...." A friend interjected saying: "We don't care which government rules, but we just want our freedom to walk about freely. How can we do it under these circumstances?" Several minutes later a second fight between two other youths started. The friend of the trader stated: "This is a fight over women. You see when you put three hens with two roosters in one pen you are bound to have trouble!" The trader added: "When the white man was in power it was peaceful here. These Blacks just take things by force and all they ever want to do is fight. What can we do? We just have to live here! We are too old to go anywhere and run away from this fuckin' country!"

In the anxiety of these tense moments a squatter approached the trader's friend to hire his truck. The purpose was to transport a load of his belongings to his rural home about 120 kilometres from Durban. In the process of negotiating the price, there were interspersed comments about the on-going fight across the road. The squatter, feeling a sense of irritation, exclaimed: "I just don't know when we Africans are going to learn to stop fighting! This is the problem everyday over here. We just can't do anything about it." This issue opened up an aspect of the wider inter-dependencies that emerged since the established of the squatter camp. Indians with vehicles, especially trucks and vans, were increasingly providing transport services for squatters, entrenching a somewhat invisible client-patron relationship. The friend stated later: "There's no problems with us here. We all get along very well. When they want to use my transport they come and ask and we settle on a good price. Because of this I am able to park my vehicles outside without problems. They know me and I stand outside late at night, they all talk to me, and nobody does me anything!" The transport was always at negotiated rates and usually paid in advance. Evidence had shown that a lucrative business was emerging between some of the Indian vehicle owners and the squatters.

The conversation at that moment turned to a revealing episode that occurred on the N2 (national coastal highway), relating to an attack that took place several kilometres away from the place of interview, a few weeks earlier. The victims were a young White couple and their two infant children who were travelling from Gauteng for a weekend in KwaZulu-Natal's north coast. As the story was reported by an interviewee:

> One of the children asked to urinate, making the father stop on the side of the road to allow the child to do so. They were then attacked by several Black youths that shot dead the father and mother. The children were then left to themselves under very cold and rainy conditions. A passing highway police patrol vehicle stopped and found the children sitting and crying on each parent. The police suspected that the murderers were from one of the neighbouring squatter camps and soon after arrested three of the suspects at about 16h00 the week before the third visit to the respective trader. The information for their arrest allegedly came from paid informants from within the squatter camp that was opposite the trader being interviewed. The arresting officers were Whites and Indians. Allegations are that the White policemen wanted to shoot dead all the three and then claim they resisted arrest, but the Indian policemen apparently did not share the same sentiment. The former's reason was based on a perception that the suspects were constantly engaged in deliberate attacks and murders against Whites.[2]

In a different episode at another trading post, the trader recalled an incident of a fatal stabbing that took place close to his operation. Information on this incident was already gathered prior to the meeting with this trader. The incident was about a stabbing which involved an Indian youth and two Black men. Attempts to reconstruct the story and ascertain the truth about what actually happened brought out six different versions of the incident, parts of which are presented in direct language:

- "You heard how these Africans were attacking the Indians in the bus this afternoon. For once the Indian boys stood up to fight them. They killed one and hurt the other one quite badly! We must stop sitting back and taking this from them. I'm glad we taught them a lesson this time."

- "Yah, last Saturday three Africans came to hold up Matthew in his shop and tried to steal his money and whatever they could lay their hands on. Some of the Indian boys were there and saw this. They caught two of them and killed one. I heard the other one is critical in hospital."
- "You know what these lighties (boys) are? They just get drunk and start interfering with innocent people. They just killed those two guys for nothing—because they were African."
- "Yah, these bastards killed my brother last year. This time they started with our guys and they didn't fright… They just fucked them up. They think we are going to be scared of them all the time! These were not the guys who killed my brother. We are still going to get them."[3]
- "Those Africans started with these lighties. They were drunk and they started interfering with the Indians. One of the lightie's had a mes (knife) and stekked (stabbed) both of them. One died same time and the other died after a couple of days. When it happened a couple of hundred Africans suddenly got wind of what happened and came fully armed and started singing anti-Indian songs. They wanted the police to do justice straight away, otherwise they were going to start attacking the Indians. When they first saw only Indian policemen, they started acting wild. The Indian cops had to call for back up, and only when the White cops came they calmed down and dispersed—but only because they were going to be tear-gased! But some of my clients from the squatter camp told me not to worry and not to close my business. They promised to stand and defend me if they attacked us."
- "Hey, these youngsters get drunk every weekend and look for trouble. They stabbed two drunken people, who I heard were old men! They made it bad for everybody now. Just and go and stand in the corner, and you won't see anybody there anymore. Why? Because they want to behave like gangsters and now they can't face up to it. The Africans are angry, and are going to attack them at night. That's why they are not coming around anymore!"

The last respondent's words about the evening gatherings were correct. Driving through the respective area over several evenings, as an observational exercise, had revealed a complete absence of youth, both Indian and African. A tense atmosphere in the area prevailed for several weeks. It brought out the historical and latent animosity between Indians and Africans. A distinct atmosphere of mutual mistrust and the fear of being attacked under the cover of darkness by either side persisted over several weeks. A nearby shop, which was converted into a billiard room and social club for the youth, mainly Indian, closed immediately after the incident. Youth from the squatter camp avoided the area, while the Indian youth gathered in the safety of several of the neighbours fenced yards. The predominant conversations among them for at least two months, was about the stabbing, the possible reprisal from Africans and how they envisaged defending themselves and their properties. Conversations often took the extreme ends of mass attacks and mass destruction by Africans, whom they believed showed their anger at such incidents only in this way. Their preparations were firstly to start with servicing of their guns, finding out about where to get more guns and ammunition, and asking the local police, who were mainly Indian, to be on constant alert. However, there was a general lack of faith in the police services, especially in view of their record of the poor ways in which they handled cases or failed to arrest culprits. One of the alleged culprits in the stabbing was arrested and released on bail three days later, while his accomplices went into hiding. The entire neighbourhood was geared into a state of perpetual readiness to vacate their homes, defend themselves and mobilise as widely as possible in order to be sufficiently prepared for a possible attack. As both groups cautiously viewed each other with suspicion, the issue calmed down after a period of about six weeks and the area returned to a semblance of normalcy. However, African and Indian youth who were on talking terms with each other either spoke carefully about the incident or avoided discussing it. They started gathering once again at their old places and the social club-*cum*-billiard room was reopened. It was a conflict that only time and cautious behaviour had helped to resolve.

The incidents and responses illustrated above are important reflections of inter-group dynamics between Indians and Africans and the manner in which socialisation actually took place in the areas of research. The nature of cordiality that existed between the traders and individuals from the squatter camps stopped at the level of acquaintanceship, hardly developing into entrenched friendships. There were various reasons for this, the main one being the unavailability of time for either party to go beyond an acquaintanceship. But there are also taboos on the part of Indians to keep out unknown people, especially if they do not belong to the same racial, ethnic or caste groups. Their social distances were not simplistically based on the aversions that arise out of possible racial or other forms of social prejudice only. However, there has been a distinct pattern of racially based socialisation among the Indian and African youth. Wherever they gathered around the traders' outlets, it was always as clearly visible groups of Indians and Africans who were in total separation from each other. While Africans communicated in their respective dialects, especially isiZulu, Indians communicated in English. Language was a distinctive barrier between the two groups of youth-helping to create and maintain specific identities within each group. Their main point of common interest was meeting friends in the vicinity of the nearest trading outlet.

Conclusion

The dynamics of trade, socialisation and general movements in the vicinities of the traders' outlets are an epitome of post-apartheid interaction between Africans and Indians. The analysis here was challenging because it mostly represented two classes which happened to be people of two major race groups in the province, one a mainly middle class segment being a distinctly settled urbanised community (Indians) and the other, being under class, showing characteristics of both rural and urban lifestyles together with a high degree of residential mobility (Africans). It was the middle-class Indians that exploited the opportunities for retail service provisions and it was mainly the under and working class Africans whose support sustained this segmented population. It was the Indians knowledge of the wholesale markets, their strong family ties and collaboration, and the advantage of operating from their private properties that made them more successful than their African counterparts. Through their additional advantage of access to capital and credit, the Indian residents-*cum*-entrepreneurs were evidently building up above average cash reserves under political and economic conditions that would generally not permit the average person to acquire. These conditions afforded them a hegemonic advantage over their African counterparts, who were seen more as sojourners rather than as a permanent part of their neighbourhoods. The entrepreneurs recognised the temporary phase in which they were operating and often commented that they had to exploit the opportunity the squatter camps presented while it lasted.

However, not all the Indian residents in the research areas were of middle class status. Many who either supported the entrepreneurs or who socialised with them were tenants and unemployed impoverished people. While all of the Indian interviewees were born and raised in Durban, they did not feel a sense of security as South African citizens in the same way that Africans felt. In the course of conversations, they often diverted from the questions by referring to their minority status, their feelings of insecurity and the difficulties of having to live their lives in constant fear. Their trading skills and fortitude in a climate of uncertainty urged them on with hope and optimism that some day in the near future they might be able to trade, walk around freely and live without feeling intimidated as an ethnic minority. These have been the profound fears of the traders and their Indian clients. While many hoped for change and relocation of the Africans to decent housing, some traders were ambiguous about this because their livelihoods depended upon the continued existence of the squatter camps.

REFERENCES

1. Interviewed several times in 1997. The particular incidents below were witnessed on 10 November 1997.
2. The information was not verified, but is used in this case to illustrate the impact of racial and ethnic divisions in South Africa.
3. The respondent of this statement was not at the scene of the stabbing when it occurred.

CHAPTER FIVE

Public Transport in Durban: Indian Privilege *versus* African Empowerment—Process and Perceptions

Introduction

In the course of researching the dynamics of the sprouting 'informal' businesses in the research areas, at least two significant incidents took place. Both incidents were about the passenger transport industry and the racial tension that prevailed between Indian omnibus operators and taxi operators, mainly African. Before I delve into the dynamics of Indo-African relations in the transport industry, a brief insight into the African taxi industry will help to contextualise the problem of competition between the two groups. Like the Indian entrepreneurs in the transport industry who took advantage of opportunities that were presented to them, African taxi operators grasped at the opportunity as private transport entrepreneurs. But it came at tremendous cost to their dignity, freedom of movement and freedom of participation in the country's economy. Khosa (1990; 1991), a South African human geographer, has discussed the total repression of the African taxi industry between 1930-1976, its limited tolerance after 1976 and final acceptance of it as a means towards facilitating the creation of a conservative petty-bourgeoisie in the African townships—in order to stem the rising tide of African radicalism. Up to a point apartheid had succeeded in achieving this by subtly coopting the South African Black Taxi Association (SABTA). The taxi industry has grown from a few dozen six-seater taxis in the 1930s to more than a hundred thousand minibuses in the 1990s (Khosa 1991: 2). By 1992 the purchasing power of African taxis had grown astronomically. They were reported to be enjoying the biggest share of the taxi-bus-train commuter service, purchasing over 800 million litres of petrol and 3.5 million tyres per annum (Khosa, 1992: 182).

Khosa largely depicts the taxi industry as 'one of the most extraordinary socio-economic phenomena in recent years' and as 'a silent revolution transforming South Africa into one of the most integrated economies' and as 'fruit of popular non-racial capitalism' (1991: 2). But the industry has not been without its problems. Khosa (1991: 18) acknowledges, but dismissively, the following: rank marshalls overloading taxis to gain lucrative favours from drivers, raising fares without consulting the affected community, commuters having to wait long queues at ranks, taxis not serving certain parts of the townships, and taxi feuding—innocent passengers becoming victims. These problems were compounded by the interviewees' responses to the taxi services and the role played in their broader perceptions of transformation in South Africa.

Indian and Coloured taxi operators were also deemed a problem, but they were not as many in number and as big a threat to the bus owners as were the African taxi operators. Numerous media reports about tension between Indian bus owners and taxi owners in the Indian townships were reported in the press, but were never raised by the interviewees. While Indian residents saw African taxis as responsible for anti-social behaviour, Indian bus owners singled them out as a threat to their livelihoods. This created a level of tension that spilled over to Indian residents who continuously complained about the unacceptable ways of the taxi drivers—particularly their flouting of traffic rules and turning most home frontages into passenger stops, in whichever area they operated. Many had also blamed the increasing car-jacking[1] and the rise of crime in their areas to the taxi industry. They also felt strongly that this would phase out the Indian owned bus service that served their populations for decades. The Indian owned bus service in Indian dominated suburbs and elsewhere were viewed with a passion by many, despite their complaints against the quality of service and the residents' complacency in dealing with it. In a 'conversation' with several residents in Clare Estate a comment was once passed about the history of the omnibus service that Indians had provided: 'My family was the first to own buses in Durban. Where the hell do these Africans come from and take over this route that we built over so many years. They just park anywhere, stop anywhere and show no respect for passing traffic. When you hoot at them they just swear at you and if you try to challenge them they are sure to shoot you!' The comment was made in the context of the violence that marked the passenger service industry at that time[2], particularly in the light of the murder of several Indian omnibus owners in recent years and the abrupt halt to which many had to bring their services.

There was a noticeable atmosphere of racial tension between Indian and African passenger service providers, with the former feeling a sense of increasing alienation in a climate of African economic empowerment. While Indian omnibus owners were licensed and legitimate operators, African taxis were not. Most omnibus owners nostalgically recalled their thriving past performances and spoke of the contemporary helplessness that they felt against African taxis, who, as one claimed with approval in a group interview, '...operate with a ruthless mob mentality. You try to challenge them and you are finished. They will 'just gang up on you.' The comment about the history of Indian involvement in passenger service and the anti-social elements that taxis brought into Indian dominated suburbs was made several times in the field, often in racially loaded statements. The frequency and passion with which these comments were made prompted an in-depth analysis into the issue, including the history of such transport in Durban.

The History of Indian Participation in Public Transport

The history of public transport in Durban was as racially based as any other public service in South Africa. Archival documents have placed on record the nature of public transport for disadvantaged citizens who lived away from the city centre in the early 1900s. Singh (1977)[3] for instance reported that up to 1919 there were no attempts to provide this facility for non-whites living in areas remote from railway or municipal tramway routes. During this period the municipality of Durban did not incorporate areas such as Clare Estate, Reservoir Hills and Overport, among a number of other suburbs, within its Borough, since they were under the jurisdiction of Local Administration and Health Boards. Phoenix at the time was not even conceptualised. Those who lived outside what was then Durban had to rely on the horse-drawn spring cart as their principal means of transport. Until the 1940s, it was not unusual for people from outside the Borough of Durban to do their shopping late in the evenings, sleep over in the premises of known people and other well meaning members of the Indian community and return home the next day (Camrie, 1985). It is not surprising that under these conditions Indians had to respond independently of the local authority public services in order to provide more convenient modes of transport for those who lived in the peri-urban areas. The idea was initially conceptualised by an Indian named Siddhoo. After seeing a Dodge truck displayed in a local garage, Siddhoo conceived the idea that if two benches were placed lengthwise in the back of the truck it would serve as a suitable mechanically powered vehicle to transport Indian and other non-White[4] passengers from outside the Borough of Durban. After borrowing money from a few friends and relatives the Dodge truck was purchased and the first Indian owned omnibus was in operation in 1919, carrying mainly passengers from Riverside, north of the Umgeni River, into the city centre. Whites were provided with public transport by the Municipality and preferred to patronise this service, especially since it operated only in their residential areas. Siddhoo's venture did not prove to be an immediate financial success, but the rapid increase of support over the months did pave the way for more people of Indian origin to enter the business. For instance, a man by the name of Marimuthu purchased an old army truck, adapted it to carry passengers and provided a service from Clairwood to the centre of Durban. Likewise, others of Indian origin began to invest in engine powered vehicles that were converted for public utility (Singh, 1977: 5).

It is from these humble beginnings that Indian owned omnibus services emerged and pioneered transport services under generally unsuitable conditions. The roads during this period were usually untarred or not serviced and went into areas that were inhabited only by non-White people. The risks and the perseverance that was shown by the bus operators had a significant spin-off for the development and extension of the Borough of Durban. Their routes serviced both the residents in the outlying areas and the businesses that fell within the Borough of Durban. In this way Indian transport operators opened up these areas for the housing of Durban's industrial workers of all races and relieved the Borough of the congestion that characterised its early development. This gradually led to plans for the Borough to extend its jurisdiction to incorporate these areas as part of its suburban residential boundaries. It also led to a policy that was aimed at giving recognition to African residential areas where African workers could live with their families and commute to work on a daily basis through public transport.

There were two factors that led to the success and entrenchment of the Indian omnibus service providers. The buses were owner-driven and serviced by themselves, and there were no garage facilities for their vehicles, leaving the owners with no option but to park them either in their properties or on the side of the road. These were significant cost saving factors that permitted the owners to structure their fares in a way that was considerably lower than the transport that was provided, especially for Whites, by the Durban Municipality. The fares were directed at the working class population, especially Indians, and were, therefore, constantly aimed at keeping them at affordable rates.

The success of these initiatives eventually led, with effect from 1 August 1932, to the dissolution of the Local Administration and Health Boards in at least seven areas, incorporating them into the Borough of Durban. They included the following suburbs: Greenwood Park, Red Hill, Durban North, Sydenham, and a large portion of Mayville, Umhlatuzana and South Coast Junction (now Rossburgh). The Borough offered several other services to these populations soon after the incorporation took place.

Unlike the reliability and consistency of the buses that belonged to the Municipality, Indian owned buses, which carried between eight and twelve passengers, varied widely in the quality of their services. In the 1930s a Commission of Inquiry into Road Motor Transportation made the following observation (Singh, 1977: 5):

> Some of the buses in operation are sound structurally and mechanically and are reasonably comfortable; but at the other end of the scale are many vehicles in a state of such decrepitude that their arrival at their destination must cause no less surprise to their drivers than relief to their passengers. But they do manage to get through even if only by good luck and with the occasional aid of a yard of wire from the farmer's fence!

Their routes up to 1930 were unregulated and without interference from any public body or the City Council. Their freedom to change routes at any time they pleased gave rise to signs such as: *'Durban to elsewhere!'* The real effect of this was that the route of the bus for any particular trip was dependent upon where the majority of the passengers were going at a particular time. But all of this had come to an end through the introduction of the Motor Carrier Transportation Act in 1930, which imposed a requirement of Motor Carrier Certificates that dictated and restricted the route that each bus could take. This Act also ushered in increasing discriminatory practices from the exclusively White City Council against the Indian omnibus owners. It filtered into the apartheid era when even more profound discriminatory practices were applied. The competition they provided to the Municipality led to sporadic outcries from the consumers of transport, both White and non-White. White outrage emerged through comparison of the fares they were being charged by the Municipality, as opposed to the fares that the Indian bus owners were charging for similar trips. This painted a picture of incompetence of the White City Councillors, whose management of public transport was increasingly brought into question by White consumers themselves. Apart from the comparatively higher fares they were being charged, the service was also allegedly running at huge losses. Indian commuters on the other hand opposed the enforcement of segregation in public transport and their inability to use Municipal buses that operated in White suburbs. In a propaganda campaign that aimed to counter Indians' objections to the policy of segregation, the Durban City Council and the Joint Wards Committee issued a pamphlet in 1946 that contained a picture of an Indian bus terminal calling it the *'Durban Indian Traffic Centre'*[5]. Immediately below was a bold caption followed by six points:

> **'Transport...European and non-European:**
> **The Durban Transport Fleet comprises 203 vehicles.**
> **Included in this Fleet are 8 trolley buses and ten single deck motor buses set aside entirely for non-European use.**
> **Out of the total fleet of 203 vehicles, 8,522 seats are apportioned to Europeans and 3,110 to non-Europeans.**
> **In addition there are 211 privately owned passenger vehicles operating (under a Government licence or concession) on non-European Services. The total seating capacity of these vehicles—an Indian monopoly entirely—is 8,230.**
> **From this it will be seen that the total seats provided for Europeans is 8,522, and for non-Europeans is 11,340.**
> **Has the Indian any complaint in this direction?**

Both the City Council and the Joint Wards Committee were clearly conflating the categories of Indians and non-Europeans as a single group. The latter was made up of Africans and Coloureds as well, who jointly outnumbered the Indian population in Durban. It was the strategy of these bodies to defend their segregationist policies and subtly deflect attention away from the ailing services they were providing in transport. Over time they tried to take over the routes that were covered by the

Indian omnibus owners. At their Tenth Annual Provincial Conference held in Durban on 22nd, 23rd and 24th November 1957, the Natal Indian Congress (Founded by Mahatma Gandhi in 1894), alleged in its Report [page 23] that

> The Council's plan to oust non-Whites out of transport business is cowardly in as much as it is vicious. This move is calculated to eradicate totally any form of competition in transport services. The Council is using its arbitrary power to cover its losses in the transport section. It is well known that through the colour bar policy in transport the Council has been showing continuous losses and it is common cause that it wishes to balance the losses by removing private competition which has been and is proving gainful through administrative efficiency and perseverance. Once the Council takes over, the efficiency in non-European transport will be wanting, especially in the distant routes, and it is especially unthinkable that the Council will continue services in corrugated roads now being served.
>
> We cannot help urging the non-European bus owners to organise themselves into a strong utility Corporation to ward off Council threats.

Numerous case histories have brought out the issue of discrimination and attempts to take over the bus services by the Council. But these efforts were not restricted to Durban only. In the neighbouring town of Pietermaritzburg and other smaller towns where Indians were providing transport for the public, similar attempts were made by White dominated Councils to take over their services. Comrie's (1985) *'Interview with Sam Chetty'* was a revealing account of how a family affected by the Group Areas Act of 1950 diverted their interests from operating a laundry to running a successful passenger transport business. From experimental beginnings in the latter venture they built up a fleet of fifty buses that serviced Indian and African dominated suburbs. The business was administered by family members who took pride in ensuring a cordial relationship with their African patrons. One sister took the role of cashier and six brothers worked as mechanics and road administrators—to minimise theft of cash from drivers and check on the quality of the roads since the Municipality did not attend to the areas that the private bus operators serviced. However, the service was ruthlessly stopped by the Pietermaritzburg Council and was sold off to a European company from outside South Africa.

In most of KwaZulu-Natal such stories of racial discrimination abound where Whites enjoyed hegemony over resources and decision making. The quest to impose Council run passenger transport services in Indian dominated areas only abated around the latter part of the 1980s when the turmoil of anti-apartheid demonstrations forced local and national authorities to focus their attention on more volatile political issues. To date, the threat to take over Indian omnibus services in the region did not resurface. But a totally different scenario has emerged in the post-apartheid era, with the taxi industry dominated by Africans, posing a new threat to Indian omnibus services and adding to the racially loaded dimensions of transformation in post-apartheid South Africa.

The Rise of the African Taxi Industry: 1977-1998

There is a need to understand the rise of the African taxi industry if the role of the Indian passenger transport provider has to be understood in the context of transformation in South Africa. Both racial segments have a history of humble beginnings and have demonstrated tremendous perseverance and positive inclinations towards market incentives. Passenger transport services have always proved to be a lucrative business, especially when they were individually or family owned. The information above has briefly illustrated how this activity has empowered a number of people of Indian origin once they became involved in it. Likewise it has been construed as a viable option for nascent African entrepreneurs. At a public seminar for African taxi operators in Durban on 2 April 1999[6], the regional Minister for Transport in KwaZulu-Natal, Sbu Ndebele, stressed that one of the quicker routes for African economic empowerment in post-apartheid South Africa is in the passenger transport industry. It was time, he stated, that African entrepreneurs captured a sizeable slice of the market, especially since this opportunity did not exist previously.

The passenger transport industry certainly proved to become a lucrative niche for Africans wanting to take advantage over the market opportunities that the unfolding post-apartheid era had brought with it. But its roots predate this era, going back to the 1960s when the most convenient mode of public transport for Africans, especially in the rural areas was the privately owned sedan taxis, especially Valiants and Chevrolets. These cars were big and spacious and were normally packed with loads that exceeded the standard six-carrier for which they were built. The service that they provided to the African population in the rural areas was reminiscent of the situation that existed in the earlier part of this century when Indian omnibus owners first began their services. While the roads in the Indian suburban areas have been upgraded and are qualitatively different from the period when they first served the population, the roads going into most of the African villages in the rural areas are still in very poor condition. Only the main arterial roads have been carefully reconstructed and provide a service for most rural people only up to a point. Many still have to walk long distances for up to two hours from the drop-off point before they reach their villages.

Since Africans were not allowed permanent citizenship in South Africa during apartheid they were also not permitted to engage in licensed business activity. Hence, any public transport that they offered was not deemed legal during this period. Their motor cars provided a service in much the same way that the earliest Indian omnibuses had done. However, this almost personalised form of service changed radically when Africans entered into the transport business in greater numbers. It goes back to 1977 when the Toyota Hi-Ace, produced as a minibus, was ushered into the market. As the fight against apartheid intensified, the restrictive laws against Africans, especially the Influx Control Laws that forbid Africans from becoming permanently urban, were being relaxed. The allowances that accompanied the relaxation of these laws encouraged Africans to enter into the transport industry. The Toyota minibus grew immensely in popularity and has become the hallmark of African public transport. Africans were previously considered a risk by the banks and were not given access to credit because of this. Many who first entered the market had done so through the capital they amassed by the use of their sedans in the taxi industry. Their ownership of new vehicles was only made possible either through self-initiative or through money that was raised through private loans from relatives and friends. It was only in the latter part of the 1980s that Africans qualified for loans from the banks, but subject to the provision of acceptable collateral. Statements were made by taxi owners and traffic officials that Toyota actually facilitated the loan scheme for Africans through negotiations with the government of the 1980s because they considered South Africa to be one of the most lucrative markets in the world for their minibus. This allegedly was a condition upon which Toyota, a major employer and supplier of vehicles, would remain in South Africa. But, in an interview with the Regional General Manager of the Company, there was an absolute denial of these claims[7].

In the course of fieldwork an interesting discussion took place with a White traffic official on the rise of the African taxi industry. His view was that

> 'The majority of taxis that operate in KwaZulu-Natal actually belong to Indian taxi owners. The Indians have been the first to run taxis in Durban, and now they have got into the Black market. Most of them use Africans as fronts for their businesses and make them sleeping partners. They buy the vehicle on the African partner's name and then pay them a pittance. That's why you see them driving so badly on the roads and overloading so much. The more they overload the more money they make for themselves. And the faster they drive on the roads the more loads they do for the day. So all the extra loads they do are for them. The owner of the vehicle just tell them to do '*x*' number of loads for the day and they want so much of money for the day. But they can't stop them from doing the extra loads because they can't control this. So the taxi driver makes more money at the end of the day. That's why I think that the state should control the taxi services. In this way we will be able to keep a proper check on who's running the taxis and make sure that everybody has licences for their taxis. Too many people just buy a combi and run a service anywhere they please. Because the Indians got more money so they buy better taxis and steal away the customers from the Africans with not so nice taxis! This is what causes the violence among the taxi people.'

The respective traffic official was a former member of the South African Police Force during apartheid (now South African Police Services). Their training was based rigidly along racial lines and was aimed to ensure the perpetuation of White minority rule. Intrinsic to such an ideology was an indoctrination process that made law and order officials believe in condescending generalisations of other racial categories. This was an important factor in sustaining White hegemony during apartheid. Hence the generalisations with which the traffic official spoke was not surprising, although it spurred on further investigation into the nature of the taxi industry.

There is an element of truth in the allegation that Indians are capitalising on the African transport routes. For instance, in at least three instances information did unfold to the effect that Indians were heavily involved in transporting Africans from the townships into central Durban and elsewhere. A major question that was raised in this situation was: *How do people with such deep historical mistrusts invest such huge amounts of money in an industry that could easily fail?* The Indian taxi owners allegedly have an innovative way of dealing with the situation. In all three cases, where information could only possibly be gained from secondary sources, Indian investors signed a formal agreement with African individuals to let them own the taxis outright after five years if they could do the following:

- bring in for instance one thousand rand per week,
- service the taxi regularly at their own expense, and
- print their own names on the driver's door to create the impression that it is the taxi drivers's vehicle.

This scheme has apparently paid substantial dividends to such owners, who persistently refused to be interviewed.[8]

But Indian taxi owners disputed the allegation that Indians are the majority stakeholders in the taxi industry and various taxi associations, which had a membership that was either predominantly Indian or African. For instance, the statistics from two taxi associations, one Indian and one African, revealed its membership as predominantly one race group or the other. Ownership of vehicles was not always a disputed factor either. The African dominated association emphatically denied that Indians were purchasing taxis for operation in African dominated routes. One official responded: *'I assure you, if this happens we will make sure that that taxi is kicked out from our association. He will never be able to run on our route because we Africans have the means to do so. We don't need Indians and Whites to come and steal our business'*. The Indian taxi association on the other hand felt likewise about the routes in which they operated. But the difference was that they were unable to block the African owned taxis from participation in their areas, although a measure of control (as discussed below) has been effective.

Within all the research areas there were minibuses and the larger regular buses providing public transport. There was also a diversity of drivers from the various racial groups, predominantly Africans,

Coloureds and Indians but no White drivers. However, their daily operations were only a semblance of coexistence. The situation was more accurately one of perennial squabbles and physical fights over rights to the municipality designated pick up and drop off points. It developed into a scenario of almost total submission by the Indian bus drivers to the African taxi operators. A number of significant changes have occurred as a result of this situation, which has shed more light on ethnic relations and perceptions of transformation.

Indian Buses and African Taxis

Tension among both sectors became apparent especially at bus stops, where taxi drivers felt an equal right to either pick up or drop off passengers. It had also become a frequent practice for taxi drivers to take over bus stops and bus terminals within the suburbs, exacerbating the tensions between bus owners and themselves. In busier routes and intersections the practice of taxi drivers has been to spend long periods in one spot in order to maximise their loads. This practice has been a source of tremendous annoyance to traffic and a major reason for altercations between bus and taxi drivers. Traffic either had to navigate its way very carefully through the meagre space left by poorly parked taxis or was often brought to a total halt. The public generally submissively permitted right of way to the taxis in order to avoid verbal abuse and possible physical attacks. The lawful rights of motorists were generally ignored and often the humblest of attempts to claim these rights have led to serious assaults and verbal abuse. Within the African taxi industry there has been numerous reports of rivalry between competing associations that has led to fatal attacks on one another. It had reached such an uncontrollable situation in 1998, that it led the KwaZulu-Natal Minister of Transport to a state of frustration, forcing him to publicly declare that *'If they do not want to co-operate and if they want to keep killing themselves then there is nothing the state can do about it!'*[9]

Indian taxi and bus owners did not escape the wrath of the violence that has plagued the African taxi industry. A number of them fell victim to the greed and control that certain individuals and associations acquired after their rapid successes in the passenger transport industry. In several suburbs across Durban the experiences of the Indian taxi and bus operators revealed a situation of a virtual siege mentality. Their years of monopoly in the transport industry was being challenged, particularly by the African taxis which brought in people from the African townships into the middle and upper class Indian and White suburbs. The entry of the African taxis into the Indian areas still meant a clear racial demarcation of the passengers they served. African owned taxis transported African passengers while Indian owned buses served mainly Indian passengers and to a lesser extent Africans. But the taxi service gradually extended into the Indian market, when passengers were being 'pinched' from bus stops, although most Indian passengers avoided the taxis. Herein lied the seeds of a racial division between the two sectors, although the buses did not substantially lose their clientele.

A survey of Indian passengers standing at several stops produced some of the following statements about their choice of transport:

> 'Do you think I'm mad? I would never take one of those African taxis. In no time my watch and bag will be taken away from me! And do you know how they drive? I'm not going to be killed by those morons! They don't have any courtesy on the road.'
>
> 'I'll never take those taxis. It's like a death wish! They just switch over from one lane to another on the freeway, don't ever indicate when they want to stop or when they take off. They think the road is just theirs.'
>
> 'No thanks. The Indian buses are cheaper and safer, although they do tend to take a little long to reach town. We would have a perfect service if only the Indian buses would keep to time.'
>
> 'I only take the taxi when I'm late for work or have to get into town faster. Otherwise I just avoid them. Even Africans avoid them, most of them prefer taking the buses. You must see the buses in the evenings—they are full with Africans.'
>
> 'I have taken the taxi a few times, but they drive like maniacs! You don't feel safe the way they drive. If you complain they just tell you to get off ! And you won't get any refund. That's why I rather take the bus.'[10]

While African taxis made a rapid thrust into the Indian suburbs by providing transport for mainly the African squatters and township labourers, they have also tried to usurp the market in a totally unorganised and ruthless fashion. Initially no procedures were followed to enter into a particular suburb. To many, if they had a vehicle it was licence enough to enter the transport sector. Application for a licence to operate in a particular area was not made by most of the operators. Numerous reports in the media attest to this situation. On 25 October 1995, the *Post*, a weekly newspaper targeting mainly the Indian population, titled a report in the following words: *'SA's Indian driving force'*. An interesting description followed thereafter:

> The small but tight-knit bus industry started by Indians in the 1930s has survived apartheid, white monopolies and ferried people who were uprooted by the Group Areas Act. Now the minibus taxis, gun toting highway men and the rising price of diesel is threatening the culture of Indian owned buses.... The Indian bus, like sugarcane, curry and rice and temples, is a legacy of the 1860-indentured sugarcane labourer from India.... Mr. Pillai, also chairman of the Clairwood-Merebank Bus Owners Association, a suburban organisation representing 28 bus owners owning 66 buses, said the tradition of Indian owned buses would not die easily. 'We have inherited the culture of serving the community from our fathers and grandfathers. Operating buses is in our blood....'

On 20 March 1997, the *Daily News* carried the following report:

> Effingham Heights sole bus operator, Mr. Amichand Ramkissoon, has hired a security company to safeguard him in his battle against 10 pirate taxi operators. Mr. Ramkissoon, who operates four buses on the Durban-Effingham route, said he had been the only provider of public transport until March 17 when 10 minibus taxis moved on to his route. 'I have been threatened with violence and this is why I have hired armed security guards to protect my buses and keep these pirate operators from working my route.'

A further report on 21 April 1997 sated that Mr. Ramkissoon had reduced his fare from R2.00 to R1.50 in order to lure passengers back to his service. But this had not worked either, despite the fact that the taxis were charging a fare of R2.20. His lack of success was not because commuters did not want his service, but because they were afraid of being attacked by the taxi drivers. Disappointingly, the Durban City Council was unable to provide him with any protection, in spite of the fact that he was the only licensed operator in the area. On several occasions, despite the security company, Mr. Ramkissoon's buses were forcibly stopped and offloaded at gunpoint by several taxis on several occasions to expropriate his load. This scare tactic broke his monopoly in the area but it did not scare him from his livelihood. However, in December 1997 one of Mr. Ramkissoon's buses was forcibly stopped by a car with three Africans, believed to be members of the pirate taxi association, and the driver, who was his son, was shot and killed instantly. Numerous other such episodes were related in the field, but with each one bringing in a specifically personal experience, highlighting the complexity of the problems between African taxi and Indian bus owners. Ethnographic data produced at least three similar stories in different routes, notwithstanding a range of other lesser-known cases. But the case study above serves to epitomise the situation of violent encounters that Indian bus owners have confronted in the passenger transport industry.

Several other Indian omnibus operators believed that they were still alive because they extricated themselves soon enough from the rapidly deteriorating routes they once serviced. The case study below for instance is an indication of how one omnibus owner survived possible attack against him.

> Z.R., a fifty-three year old omnibus operator ran a service with his late father from La Lucia into the centre of Durban for more than fifty years. The family had a monopoly for passenger transport in the suburb, which after the 1950 Group Areas Act, was declared for White residents only. But his passengers were mainly Africans who worked as domestic employees and as unskilled labourers in La Lucia's business centres. During the apartheid era Whites were not allowed to use his buses because of segregation policies. He inherited the business from his father and built upon it during the 1970s when business was thriving. From two buses he expanded to a fleet of six. Each bus began work at 04h00 and finished at 20h00 from Monday to Saturday, doing at least twelve round trips per day. At the height of their business each bus brought in between R500.00 and R800.00 per day. This lucrative route supported an extended family of at least fifteen people. Two of the buses were given to two of his brothers, both of whom were married with children. All three brothers were knowledgeable about repairs and did all their maintenance work by themselves. Up to 1993 the drivers they employed were of Indian origin. However the situation changed when circumstances demanded that they employ African

drivers, but only as a tactic than out of necessity. The events that led to this situation were typical up to the time that research for this project was stopped.

From August 1993, African taxis started ferrying workers into La Lucia. Several others joined in and eventually formed an association, although they were not licensed to operate in the area. From this point onwards the taxis adopted an offensive attitude towards his buses. Their *modus operandi* was to race in front of the buses, deliberately cut them off at the bus stops and demand that the passengers get into the taxis and not the buses. On numerous occasions accidents took place, and the reaction was to gang up and assault the Indian bus drivers and abuse them with racial slurs. This eventually led to the employment of the African bus drivers. But the same pattern of intimidation followed. At each occasion the drivers were threatened with assault and asked to warn their owner to keep out of the route. The climax to this persistent intimidation occurred when one of Z.R.'s buses was burnt and totally destroyed. He was also personally approached and threatened with violence by the taxi operators. Thereafter he decided to negotiate with the taxi association and sell all his licences to them, thereby offering to totally withdraw his services. To his surprise they agreed to negotiate and finally paid him R60,000.00 in cash for his licences. Thereafter Z.R. and his brothers sold off their buses individually. He then purchased a forty five seater luxury coach costing approximately one million rand and entered into a contract with Durban's international airport. He started a service for the tourist industry, which he claims 'is less burdensome and away from the jungle behaviour of the African taxis. I am so much more comfortable now and earning enough to meet my commitments.'[11]

A similar situation prevailed in numerous other suburbs where African workers and general consumers were ferried. Another omnibus operator made a series of bizarre claims that were nonetheless confirmed by other bus owners. For instance in routes that connect to large pockets of commuters the following incidents occurred during fieldwork:

If a fleet owner had more than one bus, but ran only one in a particular route, then during a breakdown he was not allowed to replace the immobile bus with another from his fleet. If he did so, taxi drivers would stop the bus, unload the passengers into their taxis and issue a stern warning to the driver not to return. This happened despite the fact that the replacement of one bus by another was legal.

Buses in the Newlands West route were being continuously harassed by taxis from neighbouring routes that were deliberately forcing buses off the road and off-loading them into their taxis when their routes were not paying off.

Taxi drivers were forcing Indian bus owners to increase their fares because they provided 'unfair competition.' The limited number of passengers that minibuses carried did not make their trips feasible at the costs of bus fares. Hence the bus fares had to be adjusted in favour of the taxi fares.

Buses in most suburbs no longer have the sole claim to bus stops. In fact, the taxis had usurped priority over such stops when the two met simultaneously at one spot.

The taxi industry, through the use of minibuses, had increased the national fuel import bill by thirty three per cent, according to statistics released by the National Department of Transport.[12] The Department's recommendation was to replace the minibus taxis which have a seating limit of ten, but which are overloaded to sixteen or more, with an expanded diesel powered vehicle that can seat up to twenty-two passengers. But there has been opposition from the taxis because these are apparently slower, significantly more expensive to purchase than the Toyota minibus, more expensive to maintain and will not yield the same returns because they would not do as many loads for the day. The Department's recommendation was based on figures that will save the country enormous sums of money that are lost through import bills as well as to create a safer environment for motorists.

In responding to this situation an omnibus operator retorted:

> 'Why do you think the Minister of Transport Mac Maharaj is resigning from his government position. The man is not even bothered to be relocated (*sic*) to another position in government. He knows he can't work with the African mentality that is ruling this country. He might not make a public statement about why he is resigning but this is the only conclusion I can come to. These taxis are messing up this country's roads. And if the new minister of transport is going to be an African, what is happening to education and to health in this country is going to happen to transport! There'll be no more bloody new roads after this.'

The respondent in this case belonged to a family with more than a sixty year history in the transport industry. His twenty-three years old nephew was another victim of the violence against Indian bus drivers on Friday, 23 January 1998. The story that is unfolded below brings out a number of issues that have been latent since the entrenchment of the squatter camps and the spate of house burglaries, car-jackings, assaults, and murders that have taken place in the research and neighbouring areas.

> On Friday, 23 January 1998, at about 17h00, Sudheer Debba was completing his last load for the day and was less than half a kilometre away from his home. Three African youths attempted to board his bus to go into Central Durban, but were refused entry because it was his last load. They apparently read this as a racist gesture and found it an ideal excuse to attack him. The youth then sprinted to the next bus stop and shot him several times, killing him instantly. It was alleged that a passenger, described as 'an African police reservist', took out his gun and shot at the youth to try and defend the driver. He successfully aimed at one, fatally wounding him. The other two, realising that if their injured colleague remained on the road much longer, he could capitulate and reveal their identities. They, therefore, dragged him to the nearby squatter camp and abandoned him in a shack, but against the occupant's will, and fled. Realising the legal problems of housing a fugitive, it placed the respective squatter in a difficult position, especially since she was allegedly warned by the two youths that submission to the police would endanger her life. In the meanwhile the abandoned fugitive was bleeding profusely and did not receive any medical attention for more than three hours. By that time the Indian residents had gathered around the bus and the body of the driver, trying to reconstruct the events that led to the shooting. Tempers began to flare when the passengers recollected the events of that afternoon to the family, friends and district people. An ambulance removed the body of the driver from the roadside more than two and half hours later. This long wait built up a level of reaction and solidarity from the Indian residents that brought them into a state of virtual readiness to engage in an ethnic war. Many came armed with guns, and a range of other lethal weapons, ready to extricate the alleged bleeding culprit from the respective shack, because

by then they had all learnt about his whereabouts. But it was the army that controlled the situation, after the police had failed to do so. A number of altercations took place during those highly charged moments. The first occurred between Indian policemen and the Indian residents who, as one stated, 'wanted to impose the death penalty on the bastard because the courts are likely to set him free soon after he is jailed.' The second occurred between the African and Indian policemen, when the latter was charged by the former for being too soft on the mood of the Indians. The army was, therefore, forced to intervene. At the point that the army sought to remove the alleged culprit to an awaiting ambulance, the Indian residents tried to fight their way through their cordon that surrounded it. They managed to break through and apparently almost toppled the vehicle over. When the threat of teargas and more stern action from the army became apparent, the situation calmed down swiftly and the ambulance sped off. For at least another week however, there was a conspicuous reduction of African squatters walking the streets of Clare Road, especially at night.

The solidarity that this event generated among the Indian residents was visibly binding and showed an urge as one resident stated: '*...to fight back in a way that will teach the squatters a lesson. They think we are afraid of them because they are in the majority. But this time we are going to fight, because we are tired of passively sitting back and letting them rob and murder us like this*.' For at least three weeks there was a vigilante group that operated on an informal basis until midnight. Letters were also written to the state president and the minister of police about the incident, the rampant crime and the links it had to the squatter camps within and in the neighbouring suburbs. The victim's family called a special public meeting to discuss the above issues, but it was poorly attended. However, these were no better than knee-jerk responses to a much wider and more endemic problem. At least a month after the incident an important symbolic event was initiated by Sudheer Debba's family. It was an occasion that provided an opportunity to take note of symbolic gestures from the Indian neighbourhood, the content of their conversations and its implied meanings. The event was particularly useful to observe Indian-African relations in a solemn but tense atmosphere, and to engage in an analysis of what was done and spoken in that time.

On Sunday, 22 February 1998, the parents of Sudheer Debba held a special memorial in a very unique way. They applied to the traffic department for permission to cordon off the road on two sides of the place where their son was shot, between 17h00 and 18h15, thereby stopping the traffic from both sides. The purpose was to have a *hawaan* (fire ritual) on the spot where the shooting occurred, in order to redeem his soul from his untimely death and to give his parents peace of mind that the appropriate rituals were carried out for him. The extended family, friends and the entire neighbourhood attended the event. At least three officially marked police vehicles, attended by Indian policemen only, were present. It was a noticeably solemn occasion marked by sporadic racial remarks of the senseless killing, and despite a light persistent rainfall people stood by in solidarity with the family until the end of the prayer. Africans from the neighbouring squatter camp also stood by and watched with curiosity. After the prayer all the bystanders, including Africans, were offered *prasadam* (ritual edible offerings). Many among the latter refused to accept it, while others asked questions about meaning of the event and the offerings and openly showed their remorse at the murder. While the prayer was in progress, a regular Sunday meeting was taking place within the squatter camp, from where snippets of the discussion was carried over to the prayer gathering through its public address system. In response to the meeting a bystander, standing with a small group, remarked: 'They are saying to the people in the meeting that because of criminals in the camp, all are being branded in the same way. They are going to try and sort out all the criminals they know and kick them out of the area.' Another replied: 'Ya, but these bastards got no mercy on us. They'll say they are going to do it, but nothing will happen. The stealing and everything else will continue as before. You know on that Friday night how I nearly fucked-up the cops! If we only got hold of that bastard who shot that 'lightie' we should have killed him straightaway, and the Africans shouldn't dare to do a fuckin' thing about it! We were ready. They were lucky to have the army there. Let me tell you something, we can finish this place up in one night. Some of us should just get together and start burning down all the shacks from one side and take our revenge! We can do it!' This racially loaded remark was met by a sobering response from the victim's forty three-year unmarried

> uncle: 'No, that kind of behaviour will just make things worse. You'll never enjoy killing people and destroying their things. But my spirit is broken now. I got fuck all else to live for in this country. We bought the bus for Sudheer because work was so difficult to get and we wanted to carry on our family tradition. Every weekend I used to work on his bus with him and teach him the things he didn't know. But now what's the use? I got nothing else to live for in this country—I think I'm gonna leave. My sister in Texas is calling us. My other sister's papers are already processed. But she is worried about missing her daughter and grandchildren—so she's not sure if she wants to leave this horrible country. Can you think about what pain my sister in the U.S.A. is going through right now, since she can't be with us?' Another of the bystanders contributed by saying: 'I had to sell my house in Newlands, because only Africans are buying there now. Everyday clothes are being stolen from the line and every night somebody's car is either broken into or stolen. We couldn't take it anymore. I'm lucky to get my price for my house.'[13]

The situation depicted above demonstrated a sense of helplessness among the Indian bystanders. While one was affected by continuous cases of theft in his previous area of residence, others such as the bus owners felt stifled by continuous attacks against them. But not all cases of public transport providers among Indians had fell victim to African chauvinism. Some had worked quite ingeniously to protect their routes. The difference however was not to continue their services with buses, but instead with taxis. A ploy for their survival has been to form a taxi association and to include a few African owners for good purpose, as the case study below illustrates.

> R.R., chairman of a predominantly Indian taxi association servicing a predominantly Indian suburb, once owned three buses that worked very profitably for him. By the end of 1994 he was forced to sell them off because of continuous harassment by African taxi drivers. Towards mid-1995, in his desperation to think of alternative means of self-employment, he decided to join several other Indians who were already in the taxi business and to whom he was known. He believed at this stage that big buses were intimidating to smaller vehicles such as minibus taxis because of their bigger load capacities. At the age of 48 years, he did not deem himself employable by any type of organisation,

> and neither was he inclined to because he was self-employed throughout his life. However, African taxis once again began interference in their routes, and it only stopped after a shoot-out which left one African driver dead. A truce was called and was facilitated and monitored by the local police. However, the Indian taxi owners immediately formed an association and limited the number of taxis in the area to those who were already operating in it. An exception was made for tactical reasons and they embarked on recruitment of two African taxi owners, who were well respected in the business, especially for the respect they commanded among other African drivers. The condition under which they were allowed to operate in their route was to act as spokespersons and negotiators during times of disagreements with other African taxi associations, while he and other Indian colleagues undertook to deal with other Indian associations during times of dispute. It also helped to create a semblance of multi-racialism within their association. In this way they were able to minimise the racial overtones of disagreements and succeeded in dealing with conflict resolutions in a positive manner. R.R. was happy that their approach was a workable and a safe and sensitive method of surviving in a hostile environment—judged especially by the success with which disputes were handled.

The responses demonstrated by the Indian taxi owners in the illustration above reflects a unique approach in dealing with a situation that requires racial sensitivity. There was a marked reduction in taxi pirating by other taxi operators when the association acquired legal status and were allowed to limit the number of operators in their route. The inclusion of the two African taxi owners played a significant role in reducing the existence of perpetual racial mistrust between Indian and African taxi operators. However expedient it might have been by the Indian drivers, the co-option of the African taxi owners was nevertheless an important stabilising mechanism in an area that could have threatened public transport provision, especially for Indians, if African taxi operators monopolised it. The views of Indian commuters, as illustrated above, are generally conservative and are based on perceptions that have been shaped by the predominance of bad driving and immoral behaviour and violence, particularly in the African taxi industry. Most Indian taxi owners are known to the suburban residents and, therefore, have a different measure of faith in their service. It has also been a tendency of the Indian taxi drivers to either drive the taxis themselves, employ family members or hire Indian drivers, especially for the sake of appealing to Indian commuters.

Residents, Buses and Taxis

The impact of the taxi service in the Indian suburban areas, particularly in Clare Estate and to a lesser extent in Reservoir Hills, not only affected the commuter at the bus stop but also numerous residents at their homes. When the African taxis first made their entry into these suburbs at about mid-1993, residents and bus operators made their discomfort about them known, but only informally. The early days of this service were restricted to the African squatters and were not frequent. By mid-1994, after the April 27 general election, their frequency into these areas increased rapidly. Their appearances in the areas started from humble beginnings of adhering to traffic regulations, avoiding stopping at bus stops and loading or off-loading the squatters as close to their shacks as possible. But this pattern was radically changed when the big numbers in which they operated appeared to give them a boost in confidence and they started ignoring the normal road courtesies. Any place, including bus stops and in front of houses, were good enough for them to carry on their trade, and any time was good enough to take-off, without the requirement of indicating.

Apart from the dangers that this pattern of driving introduced into these generally quiet and placid suburbs, a number of houses with accommodating driveways, were turned into convenient drop-off and pick-up points for the taxis. The affected residents were too petrified to challenge this practice either legally or personally, for fear of being attacked by the taxi drivers or their passengers. The rise in burglaries from homes and vehicles, motor car thefts and car-jackings from within people's properties, were linked by the residents to the entry of the African taxi service into their areas. After this comment was repeated several times and after listening to frequent reference to a small road off Clare Estate's main road, in which residents claimed that they were under greater siege than other residents in neighbouring roads, an examination into these claims was subsequently made. There were twenty houses on both sides of the road, which ended as a *cul de sac.* From among these houses, within a space of five months—between April and July in 1997, four people were car-jacked in their driveways, three cars were stolen from the properties and five houses were burgled.

Of the four car-jackings, two of the owners were driven away with the thieves. In the third case the owner was taken into his house, beaten and gagged, while in the fourth case the person was hit unconscious and left lying in the garage. He was found by his wife more than an hour later and rushed to hospital, where he was kept for two nights. The two who were driven away during the incidents were left in the African townships of Umlazi and Kwa-Mashu respectively, but were unharmed. All three cars were stolen at night when the residents were asleep. Two of the owners who had dogs claimed that the thieves had ingenious ways of dealing with them. For instance, in one case a bitch was allegedly brought to quieten their dog while the car was being stolen, while in the other case large chunks of meat were found in the yard, containing substances that put their two dogs to sleep. Of the five houses that were burgled, two burglaries occurred during the evening between 19h00 and 20h30. One house belonged to a panel beater and the other belonged to an affluent family business. In the former case, an ailing eighty-six years old bed-ridden woman was taunted and abused by the thieves who pulled her hair and also terrorised the children of the house. The thieves threatened to do worse if they did not get cash and a gun. The owner of the house did not own a gun, but had six hundred rand, which he gave to them. Only after pleading to the thieves for about twenty minutes, they left. In the second incident the house was attacked by four armed men, one with an AK 47 Rifle. The most senior person of the house was beaten with the gun and actually led to his safe. The thieves instructed him to open and empty it. As a businessman he was ready for such an eventuality. He had, therefore, loaded the safe with imitation jewellery, one thousand rand in cash and several thousand fake U.S. dollars. The hold-up lasted for a maximum of seven minutes. The family strongly suspected a domestic worker who recently left their employ.[14]

All of the victims were Indians, and in all the cases besides the car thefts and burglaries that occurred late at night and where those responsible were not seen, the residents identified the culprits as Africans. Hence the responses from the interviewees was produced as a 'them and us syndrome.' Their articulation of crime in the area was embedded in racial terms because it was the only way they could see it. The trauma that two women and four children suffered in three separate incidents was still visible at the time of interviews. All of them were sedated after the incidents and had taken medication for several days before they were able to calm down. None of the cars and other property that were stolen was recovered and no arrests were made for any of these incidents. In every interview, blame was apportioned to the taxis and the kind of people they carried. One response, in a sense, covers the variations of what was said about taxis and crime in eleven interviews that were done in the small road:

> 'The taxis are the cause of all the problems we have been experiencing recently. The people from the squatter camp line up here in the mornings and to a lesser extent during the day. Since there are such large numbers that stand there, when the taxis come their assistants have enough time to view our houses. They stop and U-turn on the blind-rise and just don't care about the risks. I've seen one once eyeing my house, he didn't see me noticing him. He then spoke to his friend standing outside the taxi while it was loading and pointed to my house. A couple of days later I was held up in my driveway and dropped off in Umlazi. Another taxi guy gave me a lift from there. Worse could have happened to me there. This was a quiet peaceful road and I am one of the oldest residents here. Even when there were only a few houses in this road these things never happened. Since the taxis started loading here these problems started. When they stop coming here we'll be in peace again.'

The statement above was made by an interviewee whose house was one door away from the corner house that was situated at the intersection of the two roads. The spot was on a dangerous blind-rise where numerous accidents occurred. There was no officially marked bus stop at this point because of the potential for accidents. In each of the responses, there was an expressed feeling of no confidence in post-apartheid South Africa. Apart from the crime levels and associated insecurity, the respondents generally felt that the country was seriously lacking in leadership and economic direction. All of the respondents felt a level of violation of their rights that engendered a high degree of rage amongst them and a feeling of resignation to lawlessness in a situation where the police force is deemed ineffective. One respondent claimed: "*The cop had the bloody nerve to tell me that 'You are just another statistic now! To find your car would be impossible'*." The frustration, helplessness, a quest for vengeance and the thoughts of any place away from South Africa where there is peace and security, is what characterised most cases.

Conclusion

Public transport that was provided by individual entrepreneurs in Durban's 'non-white' suburbs, has been historically associated with Indians. Many who have been in the industry for decades have grown to view passenger transport provision in racial terms. Since the earliest days of entering the market, the only competitor and obstacle to Indian bus services was the Durban City Council and the unprofitable bus service it ran for many years in White designated suburbs. The City Council's persistent attempts to oust Indian bus operators from the city's roads were also emulated by other Councils in the province. Their failure to achieve this lay in the route that they chose *i.e.* through court action. The bus owners' support from its commuters and the strong arguments that they evinced in their legal defences to remain as service providers generally won their battles against White chauvinism since 1919, filtering into the decade of the 1980s.

But the situation was radically altered by the emergence of the African taxi industry. Since the early 1990s Indian bus owners were facing a totally different kind of threat to their services, in the rising taxi industry. Unlike their White counterparts, African taxi owners forcibly claimed a stake in the transport industry. Their strength lied in their numbers and the ruthless way in which they usurped numerous routes, which were once dominated by Indian omnibus owners. They appeared to be capitalising on the undeclared motto of it being an age of African empowerment and entitlement. But to conclude that the forced entry of African taxis into Indian dominated bus routes was based on racism alone would be wrong. It would be equally problematic to suggest that this process was solely economic in that the transport sector of the region's economy provided the easiest route to facilitate African financial empowerment. The reasons are complex and would certainly include both racial and economic factors. A major factor in the transport industry is the continuous demarcation of routes along racial lines. Although there is an historical basis to this, mixed associations like the illustration given above where two African taxi owners were included in an Indian dominated association, could help to regulate, if not obliterate racially skewed perceptions of transport provision in South Africa. Such experiments, which aim to mix executive committees on racial terms and aim to protect certain sectors without room for monopolies and regulate the transport industry in more disciplined ways, could produce different perceptions of and responses to transformation in post-apartheid South Africa.

The residents' exposure to crime not only came from the taxis that ran in their areas, but it also emanated from the neighbouring squatter camp, as well as unemployed individuals who idly walked through the areas with the intention of stealing. The role that transport has played shaping the perceptions of and responses to transformation in South Africa, has been more powerful and influential than many are prepared to admit.

REFERENCES

1. Car-jacking occurs when the owners or drivers of vehicles are confronted by armed thieves and are asked to either hand over the keys of the vehicle or are asked to drive away with them. They are later either dropped off at a 'safe spot' or even murdered.
2. Between November 1997 and January 1998 two Indian omnibus owners from two prominent families who had a long history of transport services were shot and killed by Africans thought to be linked to the taxi industry.
3. Fiat Lux, August 1997—a magazine that was produced especially for the Indian population. It was often considered to be propaganda instrument by coopted members of the Apartheid regime. It has been discontinued.
4. The word is used as a convenient reference, in accordance with the literature, to people who were then not classified as 'White' or 'European'.
5. No file number. The pamphlet was part of a collection of archival documents from the Durban City Council, available for reference to researchers using the University of Durban-Westville's Documentation Centre.
6. SABC News Broadcast, 2 April 1999.
7. Interview, 9 April 1999.
8. *Ibid.*
9. SABC News Broadcast, 2 April 1999.
10. Interview, April 1999.
11. *Ibid.*, 16 April 1999.
12. SABC News Broadcast, 19 April 1999.
13. Interview, 20 March 1998.
14. *Ibid.*, September 1997.

CHAPTER SIX

Finding A New School in Post-Apartheid South Africa

Introduction

Apart from the proliferating problems emanating from the squatter settlements since the general election in April 1994, the state of education was one of the most frequently cited problems in post-apartheid South Africa. Even on the question of positive changes respondents often diverted their answers to the negative issues such as health, the virtual paralysis of the law and order apparatus, but most frequently on the issue of education. This chapter will deal with one of these issues *i.e.* education. Most respondents were despondent about the nature and rapid pace of transformation that was occurring in education. Their views were generally highly critical of both the national and regional ministries of education. Several of the central concerns were

- The premature retirement of teachers, especially from previously Indian schools, that the departments were imposing. The main objection to this was that the most qualified and experienced teachers were opting for the attractive packages that the state was offering. Its purpose, as many believed, was to replace Indian teaching staff with Africans in a situation of forced integration. The costs of these packages were also phenomenal and a major mistake, which both national and regional departments eventually acknowledged.
- Admission of African pupils into Indian schools from the neighbouring squatter camps and African townships. The problem with this was that they were not fluent in English, thereby stifling progress in the classroom of better prepared

Indian children. Many were also travelling long distances in arriving at school after it began.

- Lack of decisiveness from the regional and national ministries of education—especially in provision of adequate numbers of teachers, lack of funds for proper maintenance of the schools, and undercutting overall budgets for school facilities.
- Accusations of corruption within official circles and the lack of a proper conceptual focus on educational policies.
- A general breakdown in morale and commitment within the education fraternity, both regionally and nationally.
- Lack of discipline among school pupils and the inability of teachers to effect meaningful disciplinary measures against unruly pupils because of the abolishment of corporal punishment.

On numerous occasions the issue of the educational system during apartheid was recalled with nostalgia. In one instance the spouse of a leading teacher activist who died in 1996, recalled her husband's warning to the future generations of Indians in South Africa. She stated: "Just before his death, my husband started taking a different view of education in the future South Africa. From what he saw was happening in education, I have heard him say to many friends who visited him or who spoke to him over the telephone, that while they fought hard against apartheid education, it is unfortunately going to be worse in the new South Africa. He acknowledged that what we used to have under the Department of Indian Affairs is going to outshine what the ANC has to offer."

Likewise, there was continuous reference to the history of Indian education and the trials and tribulations that it underwent since its formative years in South Africa. Older, retired teachers, whose contribution to primary and secondary education was offered under different political, economic and social conditions, painfully remembered the issue. In numerous instances interviewees expressed a strong desire to have their histories in education recognised by the state, in order to be party to the pace of transition in education.

The History of Indian Education

There has been a strong tendency by the interviewees to see Indian education in South Africa as being started by Indian pioneers alone.

There was a passion with which many tended to argue about achievements among Indian students and the humble backgrounds from which many came. Words to the effect: "We Indians started our own education ourselves" and "We built our own schools....", was often expressed in anger about their perceptions of the contemporary state of education and past accomplishments, especially in view of the high premium that Indians placed on education. Palmer (1957: 165) reported that the government was very slow in erecting schools for Indians. In 1954-95 90 per cent of Indian schools were government aided, with major expenses borne by the Indian community. In 1951, the Natal Indian Teachers Society undertook to raise 150,000 pounds, with 25,000 pounds contributed by themselves. Out of 1500 teachers, 1000 Indian teachers agreed to a levy of 6 per cent of their salary for one year, with the option of contributing it over two or three years.

But this called into question the actual origins of the provision of Indian schools in the colony of Natal. There are various reports of how this actually began, although the real situation is one that has been initiated and sustained by Whites, not too long after the arrival of the first Indian indentured labourers in 1860. The first attempt to set up a school was made by Father Sabou, from the Church of South Africa in 1863. But his first application for funds from the colonial authorities was turned down. Father Sabou persisted in his efforts to provide education for Indian children and subsequently opened a private school in 1867 with thirty pupils. In the same year this was followed by Reverend Ralph Stott from the Wesleyan Mission, who established two schools, one a day school and the other an evening school. Their efforts were eventually rewarded when the colonial government demonstrated their recognition for the schools by granting each of them twenty-five pounds to support their efforts. Soon after, schools were established by other missionaries and well-meaning colonists in Umkomanzi, Sea Cow Lake, and Umzinto.[1]

Although the efforts to provide schooling facilities had spread, it was only out of goodwill among individuals and in some cases it was a subtle attempt in order to get them to read the Bible and to convert Indians to Christianity. There was no official attempt to provide schooling for Indian children. At that time the primary aim was to provide labour for the sugar estates and in other areas where it was required, such as in the railways and coal mines. In 1877, the Protector of Indian Immigrants declared:

> No systematic effort has even yet been made for the education of the children of the Indian immigrants of the colony.... And I am inclined to think that more satisfactory results will be achieved by this means than would be likely to attend any missionary effort in the same field, and that the whole resources at the disposal of the government for this purpose should be directed to the support of its own student schools.[2]

This well-intentioned statement did not have the impact that the Protector intended it to have. There was an increased rise in anti-Indianism by Whites during this period and the special provisions set out by Law 20 of 1878 to cater for the suggestions of the Protector, turned out to be inferior and minimum provisions. It perpetuated the disparity in education with what was then provided for the European community. However, a degree of expansion did take place soon after. The two schools that were started by the colonial authorities in 1879 increased to twenty-six in 1894.[3] But education, up to that stage, was only offered up to standard four (six years of primary schooling). In the same year the Indian Immigrant School Board was abolished and replaced by the then Department of Education. Through this structure there was more consistent and organised efforts to address the issue of schooling for Indian children. The first time secondary education was offered to Indian children was in 1899. Thereafter, a number of other schools were set up to meet the needs of the offsprings of the growing indentured population. In 1909 the Natal Government appointed an Education Commission which recommended that "*in districts in which this class of our population is most congested Government primary schools should be established.*"[4] After much agitation by South African Indians and the Government of India against anti-Indian behaviour, the famous 1927 Cape Town Agreement that was concluded between the Union Government and the Government of India. They agreed in principal, *inter alia,* that "*.... In the provision of education and other facilities, the considerable number of Indians who will remain part of the permanent population, would not be allowed to lag behind other sections of the community.*"[5] Numerous historical reports, including those referenced below, have illustrated generally positive responses from Indian parents in the advantage they took of the opportunities in schooling for their children. Although statistics show that girls attended schools in smaller numbers in the formative years of Indian schooling, contemporary data reveals that the present situation has reached gender equality, and in numerous other cases the situation with the female component is much higher than the male component.

From these humble beginnings and the successes and achievements that were witnessed in the history of Indian education, there has been numerous tributes paid to the Indian population for them. For instance, an inspector by the name of Mr. C.T. Loram felt compelled to place on public record his observations:

> Whatever view may be held as to the desirability of educating these people, it is impossible not to admire the efforts of the Indian teachers towards self-improvement, both in general and professional knowledge. *(Ibid.—Natal Mercury Supplement)*

Writing for the same edition, the Administrator of Natal, Mr. T.J.A. Gerdener, said in the opening of his tribute:

> There is no gainsaying the fact that the most important single reason for the progress made by Indian South Africans over the past decade should be sought in the tremendous importance which they as a group attach to the education of their children.

It was in comments such as the above that many respondents appeared to have forgotten the role and accomplishments of the missionaries and the colonial authorities in Indian education. Their focus was essentially on two issues. First, they paid more attention to schools that were started in the earlier part of the twentieth century by affluent community spirited Indians. These schools were later assisted by the state and referred to as "state-aided" schools. Second, influenced by the concept of state-aided schools, they paid selective attention to what was achieved under trying circumstances and with minimal domestic resources among many Indian families. It was from this early period of perseverance and fortitude among poorly equipped children and grandchildren of indentured labourers that a formidable educated Indian middle class emerged in the decades that followed. As the years went by there was an equal amount of progress with the educational levels towards which Indian children were aspiring. Teaching was widely considered as a high status job in the Indian population until the early 1980s. Any person aspiring towards becoming a teacher was often instantaneously bestowed with respect and admiration within the community. It was a well protected job offered by the state, with attractive benefits and all those who qualified with teaching degrees or diplomas were guaranteed employment—but in Indian schools only. This privilege has come to a virtual halt as transformation in education begins to tackle the mammoth task of undoing the four decades of prejudice during the apartheid era. The initial attempts after the general election in April 1994 has set the government out on a road of continuous confrontations with the educational fraternity at large and consistent outcries of no confidence from the public in their strategies to restructure education.

The Present State of Schools in Three Areas

To understand the contemporary situation in the once Indian dominated schools in predominantly Indian suburbs, first requires an insight into some of the contemporary problems that have affected education throughout South Africa since the 1994 general election. The bumpy road of educational transformation in the country led to several significant decisions by the Ministry of Education that has paved the way for radical changes to take place. In order to level the fields among the four designated racial groups *viz.* White, Indian, Coloured and African, the state has been forced into a situation of extreme difficulty in re-working the budget for this important aspect. In simple terms, those population categories that were previously privileged with better funding and facilities, especially Whites, and to a lesser extent Coloureds and Indians, were no longer going to enjoy the same. Priority, and rightly so, had to be re-directed to the most disadvantaged segment in the country *i.e.* towards Africans. South Africa's expenditure on the education budget is deemed to be one of the highest in Africa, comprising a significant proportion of the country's total annual budget. Despite this, the task of repairing past damages, incurred during apartheid, have proved to be more difficult than initially anticipated. This is because of a wide range of problems, especially, as identified by the interviewees,

- the ANC's inexperience in government and their forced reliance upon administrators who still had solidarity with the previous apartheid government,
- pilfering and mismanagement of funds and resources by ANC inclined and other African government officials,

- a widespread lack of accountability, as seen for instance, in the construction of a new school in Ulundi which cost thirty-three million rands and which was commissioned by the Inkhata Freedom Party appointed Minister of Education in KwaZulu-Natal, and
- ill-conceived policies such as retrenchments, redeployments and affirmative action that have had a major negative impact on education throughout the country.

These aspects are the major points of concern to education upliftment and stabilisation in the entire educational fraternity in the country.

Ill-conceived policies have been identified by many of the respondents, critics of education policies and the media, offering severance packages to the most experienced and productive teachers in KwaZulu-Natal, forced redeployment of teachers to rural areas and African townships, and forced integration of schools. Each of these issues has contributed to a situation of uncertainty, insecurity and unhappiness in the education fraternity at large. Several hundred teachers, especially Indians with proven experience, had accepted the severance packages because it was so attractive. But the idea backfired, although the state could not rescind it decision because of the legalities that were involved. It was common to hear teachers who were interviewed express dissatisfaction with almost every aspect that they chose to discuss about the confusion in education and how they are linked with the perceptions of deteriorating conditions in the country. Integration was proving to be a particularly difficult issue to handle. One teacher once exclaimed, when asked what she thought of the new changes in education:

> Asking me about school is like asking me about the conditions in the country. We try so hard to teach the children in this school and it is simply not appreciated. Now we have 80 per cent African pupils in our school, which was once an all-Indian school. We were looking forward to teaching African pupils in the 1980s when we tried to defy apartheid and had this utopian idea that integration is the best way to solve apartheid's discriminatory policies. But the reality now is different. Most of the African students in the classes are way over age. So the Indian pupils who have kept up their education over the years and passed are just

> snowed under and bullied by the bigger African pupils…One day in one of my lessons two Black boys went to the back of the class, sat on the trestle and kept kicking the students in front of them. After telling them several times to stop it, I just got fed up and walked out of the class. This is just a mild incident in comparison with other incidents that have taken place in the school.

Another teacher from the same school stated:

> You know yesterday I gave a test to one of my classes. One girl wanted the answers to the questions from the boy sitting next to her because she didn't learn. When he kept refusing, she got up and punched him in the nose, then kicked and slapped him! She was so big size the poor boy couldn't do anything, and I was too frightened to get in between! There is such a lack of discipline in this school that you may never believe the problems we go through. I have taught Indian pupils for more than twenty years and I have never come across something like this. The problem is that these students come from broken homes and the townships where they live there is only violence. So the kind of dedication that Indian students have to their work is different from the Africans. If it carries on like this I will have to give it up.

In another school where the demography had changed from being entirely Indian to 40 per cent African, a teacher remarked:

> Indian and African students just do not get along in this school. They form gangs and we know they are armed and ready to fight with each other. The biggest problems we experienced since this school was integrated was the interference of Indian girls by African boys, and in between lectures they just take their own time to walk from one class to another. At least ten minutes are lost in each period, because it is fun for them to taunt the teachers by walking slowly and taking their own time. Now we can't discipline the Indian students anymore because they just ask us "What about them?". They know we are powerless now because we can't punish them anymore.

The problems expressed in these statements are rooted in the rapid pace of integration that has taken place in South African schools. In the Greater Durban Region Indian schools were flooded by an influx of African pupils from the neighbouring townships and squatter settlements. Many African pupils have been reported travelling up to thirty kilometres by bus in the mornings, leaving home at a 06h00 to reach their schools by 07h30. But very often they do not make it in time. Other children from the squatter settlements often attend school poorly fed, without lunches and not in the cleanest condition, because of the lack of water in their places of residence. But it was evident that most African children were trying to appear neatly attired when they went to school, although their performances showed out glaring class differences between themselves and their Indian counterparts. Within a period of two years, most schools in the suburbs of Clare Estate, Overport, Reservoir Hills and Asherville have transformed from being entirely Indian. Table 6.1 indicates the number of pupils by race in eleven schools in April 1999. The odd school in the table is Rippon Primary, which was during apartheid an all-Coloured school. The purpose of including it was to illustrate the meagre shift of Indian children to such a school as opposed tc the major shift to formerly all-White schools.

Table 6.1: Illustrating pupil population by race category in 11 schools in three suburbs *viz.* Clare Estate, Reservoir Hills and Asherville, 1999. The first and second figures in each column represent boys and girls respectively.

School	*Indians*	*Africans*	*Coloureds*	*Whites*	*Fees*
Palmiet Primary	75; 73	224; 198	8; 3	0; 0	R275.0
Clareville	19; 12	131; 112	0; 1	0; 0	R100.0
Resmount Primary	98; 127	160; 170	2; 4	0; 0	R300.0
Hillview Primary	45; 29	88; 137; 10	0; 2	0; 0	R300.0
Clayton Primary	195; 194	182; 153	5; 9 (14)	0; 0	R300.0
S.M. Jhavary Primary	211; 207	69; 55	16; 4	0; 0	R300.0
*Rippon Primary	4; 7; 31	279; 331	176; 162	0; 0	R200.0
Centenary Secondary	469; 371	45; 70	9; 4	0; 0	R400.0
Reservoir Hills High	393; 358	68; 82	9; 9	0; 0	R685.0
**A.D. Lazarus Secondary	800	300	0	0; 0	R300.0
Burnwood High	318; 305	266; 210	25; 22	1; 0	R476.0

* Rippon Primary is a formerly all-Coloured school, with 3 Indian teachers and 22 Coloured teachers.

** This school has taken a principled stand in not doing the racial statistics because their view was that all children should be considered as "learners", irrespective of past racial classification. The figures given for Indians and Africans are only estimates.

It is clear from Table 6.1 that radical changes have taken place in schools that were once forbidden to enroll children who were not officially classified as Indian/Asiatic. Only one of the Indian schools *i.e.* Palmiet Primary, had an African teacher. The others were still entirely staffed by Indians. In all of the schools the African pupil enrolment increased significantly. Most of them were either from the squatter camps that were situated within the respective suburbs or not resident in the suburb at all. The statistics above provide a stark contrast with the figures that were produced from the earlier records in education that was available to the Indian population. In 1894, the estimated number of school-going children in the Greater Durban Region was approximately 10,000. But the total attendance at schools was recorded at 1,581, attending at least 24 schools. This provided an average of 66 pupils per school. If each of the schools Table 6.1 have been designed for more than 500 pupils, an important question arises: Where are all the Indian children gone to if the former all-Indian schools now have so many African pupils? The answer to this question can be easily found in the previously all-White schools that were in the suburbs neighbouring the research areas, and even further away. Westville, designated for White residents only during apartheid, was one of the closest suburbs to the research areas, while suburbs such as La Lucia and Umhlanga Rocks were much further away.

Before the issue of a shift away to the White schools by Indians is discussed further, there is a need to first identify at least two groups here. One is the group of parents who still patronise Indian schools and the other that has shifted patronage to White schools. Those parents who kept their children in Indian schools had done so for at least one of the following reasons:

1. The school fees in the White schools were too high.
2. Difficulties in transporting children to far away White schools, which added to the cost of travelling.
3. The Indian schools close by were convenient and offered a reliable education.
4. Trust in the Indian teachers to enforce discipline and teach with the passion of the past when Indian schools were noted for the control they enforced on student behaviour.
5. Did not really know the difference between White and Indian schools, and were relatively unaffected by it.
6. The need for their children to have exposure to African

children, since this will be the future with which Indians will have to adapt.

Individuals who were in the minority among the interviewees made the last two points. Eight parents, all of whom were renting either in outhouses or in part of a larger house, were of humble backgrounds with little education themselves. Their occupations were mainly in low-paid employment such as in factories, the municipality, and casual labour in places like shops and service stations. They were neither politically alert nor articulate in the changes that were taking place around them, although they appeared to be generally antagonistic and afraid of the reality of having an African dominated government. It was also apparent that the children were not receiving the guidance and stimulation in their education that their better-off counterparts were receiving. While parents hoped for better performances from their school-going children, the effect of their poor means and limited aspirations—conditioned by their own lack of education—appeared unlikely to urge them on into academic or professional careers. Their own lack of self-confidence in a sense contributes towards the reproduction of a lower educated under-class segment.

To seven of the eight, the future was frightening and the prospects for their improvement appeared to be nil because of this reason. Their perceptions were based on sources of information that were derived mainly from what they were hearing from their employers and others with whom they spoke or overheard. Only one of the eight was positive in the sense that he had a light hearted attitude and had no inhibitions about who he or his family associated with. To him *"We are all one, we are all human. We must live together."* On the other hand, the protagonists of the last numbered reason noted above were on the opposite end of the group. They were twenty-three among the total number of interviewees who were within the range of middle-class households, from professions such as teaching, lecturing, working in banks and the police force and other white collar jobs. All of them had given confident and optimistic answers about the schools to which they sent their children. Their responses were articulate and reflective of a segment that was prepared to accept the country and its government for what it was. To them the problems were easy to understand and accept and ought to be seen in the light of a painful period of transition from a race based society to a fully democratic and non-racial one. They firmly believed that the schools that their children were attending were preparing them for the unfolding democracy and equal opportunities that will eventually dawn upon the entire country. Their optimism was in sharp contrast to the majority of interviewees, especially those who sent their children to White schools.

Table 6.1 alludes to an earlier point that there has been a tremendous shift in school enrolments by the various population groups, with Indian parents enrolling their children in more expensive previously all-White schools, while African parents have focussed largely on the lower fee-paying previously dominated all-Indian schools. At least 60 per cent of all the teachers who were interviewed were sending their school-going children to what used to be referred to as "Model C" schools. This phenomenon was started in the early 1990s by White schools in order to protect themselves from an influx of children from other population groups before apartheid could be dismantled. Their method of controlling this influx was to substantially increase the school fees, administer special tests to children of other race groups before entry and to restrict pupils to the suburbs in which the school was located. The second phenomenon was a particularly humiliating practice for Indian children and parents to go through, although many resigned to accepting it. The common reason for this transference of Indian children was that parents perceived former Indian schools as becoming too untenable through the increased enrolment of African children. One major problem was the slow pace at which teachers felt compelled to teach—in order to keep pace with the African children whose first language was not English. Among the Indian children, English was the spoken language, which gave them an advantage over their African counterparts. Another problem emanated from the racially based perceptions that many Indian parents harboured. In this instance the issues of lack of discipline, possible violence against their children and sexual harassment of girls by African boys, were major concerns to at least thirty-seven of the interviewees who expressed concern about allowing their children to remain in Indian schools.

The problems with indiscipline in general in Indian schools have become a source of major concern to many parents. This sentiment was derived from personal experiences that were reinforced by the media that frequently reported on the extensive lack of discipline and progress by both teachers and pupils in African schools. None of the interviewees had ever been to African township schools, but had relied upon such reports alone. Others among the total number of interviewees were not as emphatic about the indiscipline and sexual harassment as the thirty-seven who are noted above. But many did allude to these problems in more indirect ways. To such interviewees it was the responsibility as parents or family to ensure that the children got a decent education, and for them that was best located in the domain of previously all-White schools.

The issue of cultural and racial diversity brought about fear and anxiety in the quality of education in their neighbouring schools and prompted parents to search for alternative institutions. Although many respondents saw their major problems as an "Indian-African dilemma", the problem was much wider than this. Intolerance and non-acceptance across the spectrum of schools have become a major problem. The inability to deal with cultural norms of different religious and ethnic groups and the insensitivity with which they were handled have led to serious misunderstandings that were construed by many as acts of racism. The media carried several reports on this problem. For instance, in two separate editions across a period of two years, two striking headings appeared in one of KwaZulu-Natal's most widely read weekend tabloids: **"Culture shock: Teachers say they are ill-equipped to cope with mixed classes" and "Integration at schools need greater study".**[6] *In the first report some of the things that were reported showed consistency with what interviewees were saying:*

> Teachers at former Indian schools say they are having difficulties which stem from their failure to communicate with pupils, the breakdown of discipline in classrooms and an inability to bridge the gap between teaching Indian and African pupils. Interviewed this week, school principals and teachers from Chatsworth, Isipingo, Reservoir Hills, Effingham and Phoenix, said they did not object to having mixed classes, but they felt they were ill-equipped to cope with the demands of African pupils....Parents, pupils and teachers from homogeneous groups were suddenly expected to interact with other groups....In the past there were departments with qualified counselours and guidance teachers trained to provide such services. Owing to rationalisation, the infrastructure for such services had collapsed.

In the second report, the broader issues of cultural intolerance and problems of integration in schools that did not have large numbers of African students were covered. It focussed on the complexity of integration and the need for an infrastructure that will address the requirements as they arise. It recognised three issues that would require careful sensitive attention *viz.* multi-cultural, multi-linguistic and multi-religious pupils, in order to deal with the ingrained racism that is so prevalent in South African schools. In 1998 a number of incidents occurred that raised public awareness and the need for these measures. At least four incidents have been recorded (*Sunday Tribune,* 16 June 1996) where it did not have anything to do with indiscipline of African pupils, as it had to do with perceptions from people of different racial backgrounds:

- In November 1998 an Indian pupil from the famous Northwood Boys High School, previously all-White, shot and killed himself. A note that he left behind inferred that his unhappiness at school led him to do this. His father blamed it on racial intolerance at the school, although the pupil's record was not, according to the school, entirely clean.
- In October 1998 a Sotho pupil from Westville Boys High School, previously all-White, was stopped from attending school after he had shaved his head in a symbolic mourning of his grandfather's death. The school later rescinded their decision against the boy and apologised to his family.
- In September 1998 a group of Muslim pupils allegedly stabbed an Indian Christian pupil at Newcastle High School while he was practicing on the piano in the school's music room.
- Also in Newcastle in September 1998, a seventeen years old Indian pupil allegedly stabbed another Coloured colleague to death after school hours and outside the school premises. The fight was apparently started on racial grounds.

Although these issues are clearly outside the sphere of African influences, the perceptions by many respondents was these incidents still fall within the ambit of the ANC/African dominated government in South Africa since April 1994. There was a mixed set of reactions in how people expressed their disappointments since this period. While some saw the breakdown in discipline as a result of the new approaches to education, most others associated this with the new government. More intimate discussion on the issue often gave rise to more crude forms of description of the inabilities of "African governments", often by referring to the breakdown of civil societies in other parts of the African continent. Countries such as Somalia, Ethiopia, Democratic Republic of Congo, Rwanda, Burundi and Mozambique were often cited as justifications for their beliefs and lack of confidence in the future of education in South Africa. Apart from these, Uganda was a particularly frequent reference in this case in that the delivery of public services virtually seized when Idi Amin took over the country and expelled all the Indians in the 1970s.

The interviewee, who drew attention to the four instances of violence above, was an ex-teacher and an activist against apartheid and within the teachers union who studied to become a lawyer. At the time that he had planned to resign from teaching, the state offered severance packages to teachers, which he immediately grasped at because it was financially more rewarding for him to resign in this manner. He had a mature understanding of political developments in South Africa and how the formulation and implementation of policies affected a minority such as Indians, especially in education. He summed up the situation in the following words:

> You see for years we Indians were protected under apartheid and the Department of Indian Affairs. Throughout this period they only saw education in terms of segregated facilities and only Indian teachers teaching in Indian schools. Now the state is trying to make room for more Africans to enter into schools all over the country and for more African teachers everywhere. The policy is to integrate the staff at schools as well, which is inevitable if we want change. This is what we've been fighting for all these years. But I understand the problems of many Indians. So many children come from squatter camps who can't speak English, the best of Indian teachers and administrators have opted for the severance package, teachers are not adequately trained to effect the Education department's new policy of '2005', and say what you will, but the African teachers don't have the commitment that Indian teachers have in teaching the children. The lack of commitment in the township schools is ample demonstration of this. So there will be a lot of problems in transformation and on-going cultural conflicts that are going to take unpleasant racial turns from time to time. We must expect this. So for those who want to remain in this country, they must start thinking positively and contribute to change. It will work.

This statement only ended in a positive note, but it tacitly acknowledges the confusion, frustration and anxiety that are so prevalent under the present system of education in South Africa. Despite the widespread drop in moral and dissipating confidence in the Education ministries, the state has refused to acknowledge these factors as emanating from their style of leadership. The responses that this project collated were significantly consistent with a survey that was conducted and published in April 1999 by an industrial psychologist, Dr. Louise Holman.[7] Her data showed that more than half of the teachers and principals who did not accept the severance packages previously offered by the state, would leave the profession if they could. She deducted from her information that levels of motivation plummeted by a staggering 37 per cent, after establishing the five motivational factors for teachers *i.e.* children's behaviour, extra curricular activities, effectiveness of school leadership, no red tape and team work coupled with communication. Assessments of these factors also detected a sharp increase in violence between pupils, and disobedience coupled with decrease in honesty. The state's response was to deny validity of this report by questioning its methodology and threatened Dr. Holman with legal action if she published the report. These factors harp upon the reasons that so many parents of Indian origin are sending their children to schools outside their suburban areas, despite having schools nearby.

Looking Out—White Institutions as a Solution for the Best Education

Making a choice for the schools or tertiary institutions which parents made for their children was a careful, time-consuming and often costly exercise. It was a decision that was made with a strong passion and a determination to facilitate children into fields that is not only secure but also which has an important element of comfort and status in it. While in retrospect, the statement in the *Natal Mercury Education Supplement* (September 28, 1965) by the former Administrator of Natal, Mr. T.J.A. Gerdener, that Indians as a group attach tremendous importance to the education of their children, could reliably be read as a justification for segregated education, the ethnographic information certainly alluded to this factor. But the decision was not derived out of sheer racism. Recent media accounts as well have demonstrated this factor. For instance, a prominent medical doctor who wrote for the *Independent on Saturday* (24 April 1999) reiterated the importance that Indian parents attach to the education of their children. The article was in response to the huge bribes that Indian parents were paying to officials of the Medical University of South Africa (MEDUNSA), for enrolment of their children. The amounts ranged from R45,000.00 to R90,000.00 per year. In response to this situation, a general practitioner was quoted as saying: "Status in the Indian community is a big issue. There is always pressure from the immediate family and relatives for the offsprings to follow in the same path as their parents, especially in the case of doctors or lawyers. Only professionals like doctors, lawyers, teachers and chartered accountants were considered to be socially acceptable in the Indian community. If you chose one of those careers, only then would you get more respect and automatically, more attention." Another doctor added: "Indian students, unfortunately, previously didn't have many successful engineers, architects, musicians or sportsmen to look up to as role models. All the successful and well-respected professionals in the community happened to be medical doctors." Most of the middle-class to more affluent households lacked the confidence of schools run by Indian staff and attended by mainly African pupils. Their confidence was not lost in the Indian teachers and principals as much as it was lost in the forced and swift integration of the schools and in the regional and national ministries of education. Their major concern, as reflected in a number of responses, was, apart from the issues noted above on indiscipline, the fear of their children lagging behind in general academic progress. This arose out of the perception that African children were not ready to cope with the standard and discipline that Indian children are used to. Formerly Indian schools, being still entirely subsidised by the state, also had larger numbers of pupils, and were seen as lacking in discipline. Formerly White schools were seen as being more disciplined and were able to keep the classes in smaller numbers, thereby affording the children better attention.

In at least 106 households of the 255 interviewees, there were children attending once all-White institutions—primary, secondary and tertiary. Schools were a particularly difficult arena to enter into if the incumbent was from outside the suburb. A number of parents were adamant about their children not attending the district schools because they had too many African pupils. Their reasons ranged from a mixture of outright ethnocentrism to shifting their children to predominantly Indian-pupil populated schools—but which were in White areas and complemented by almost all-White staff. From the minimal information that the broader questionnaires produced on families making a choice for their children's education, an arbitrary figure of twenty households were selected to gather more information on how, why and when the decisions to send their children to the formerly all-White institutions were made. Table 6.2 illustrates some of the factors that were pertinent in collating the information to address these three questions.

Table 6.2: Illustrating household number (1), number of school-going children (2), distance between home and district school (3), approximate distance between home and the school/institution attended (4), the fees per child in the nearest district school/tertiary institution and average cost per child in the formerly all-White school respectively/tertiary institution (5).

1	*2*	*3*	*4*	*5*
1	3	200 m	15 km	R300; R3900
2	1	500 m	21 km	R300; R2600
3	3	700 m	12 km	R300; R3200
4	2	300 m	16 km	R275; R2800
5	2	1 km	6 km	R300; R2800
6	2	400 m	9 km	R300; R3600
7	1	50 m	15 km	R100; R4200
8	2	600 m	17 km	R100; R2800
9	2	1 km	13 km	R275; R3200
10	2	400 m	15 km	R275; R3000
11	3	100 m	15 km	R300; R2900
12	2	300 m	12 km	R275; R2800
13	2	300 m	5 km	R300; R2800
14	2	700 m	10 km	R200; R2600
15	1	3 km	17 km	R8500; R9350
16	1	5 km	15 km	R9000; R10210
17	2	2 km	15 km	R9000; R11200
18	1	7 km	16 km	R9000; R11200
19	2	7 km	Pretoria	R9000; R21000
20	1	4 km	C.T.	R9000; R23000

Numbers 1 to 15 reflect the houses which sent their children to previously all-White schools, while numbers 15 to 20 reflect those houses where children were attending formerly all-White universities. With respect to the school-going children it is apparent from Table 6.2 that everyone of them had access to schools that were walking distances from their homes and which required school fee payments that were significantly lower than what the former all-White schools required. There is between 1000 and 1500 per cent difference in school fees in all of the cases cited in Table 6.2. In addition to the enormity of the school fees, there is an added cost of transporting the children to and from school. This amounts to an average of an additional R1800.00

per annum per child in each household that relied upon a paid service. In cases where transport was not arranged through a service provider, there was an additional responsibility of parents and other family members having to interrupt their daily duties in order to drop-off and pick-up school children. Only individuals whose children were fetched by retired parents or housewives expressed any measure of comfort and convenience in this situation.

In the last five cases the choice of the tertiary institutions were equally important in how parents and children made their choices. In all of these cases the courses that the students chose to do at the universities in which they were studying *i.e.* at the Universities of Natal (Durban), Pretoria and Cape Town, were alsc offered in the university that was closest to them, *i.e.* at the University of Durban-Westville. Yet they chose to register in universities that were previously all-White and where the costs were considerably higher than the University of Durban-Westville. In the cases that reflect Pretoria and Cape Town, the costs increased by an additional R10,000.00 and R12,000.00 per annum respectively in order to cover living expenses. The justification for these choices was made in responses such as: *"They are getting a better education at Natal University..."; "There's too many boycotts and too much violence at Durban-Westville"; "The Blacks have messed up the place at Durban-Westville. It's too dangerous for my children to study there."* These statements were made with spontaneity and the antagonism against the University of Durban-Westville only partially subsided when the interviewees realised that they were responding to a member of staff from the institution. There was a visible sign of pride in most parents who spoke about the university that their children were attending. Their financial and domestic obligations in this regard were only secondary to them. It was the joy of seeing their children being educated and in so doing keeping up the family name and dignity. Whether their assumptions of student misbehaviour and standards being lower in the University of Durban-Westville were correct or not, was hardly a matter of concern to such households. They held on to the prestige and reliability that the former White universities appeared to bestow upon them.

Networking—Kinship, Neighbourhood and Friendship as Resources

In the search for schools and tertiary institutions parents often sought advise and assistance from their kin, neighbours and friends in choosing a school for their children. The requirement that children wanting to attend previously all-White schools be resident in the respective suburbs, posed a problem for most parents who wanted to send their children to these schools. In order to seek admission Indian parents were asked to produce proof of their property tax receipts, telephone and electricity bills, together with their and their children's identity documents. In addition, the children were subjected to performance and psychological assessment tests that were actually not an official requirement. But parents who resided outside the suburbs chose not to challenge the situation for fear of being found out and possibly victimised for taking a stand. For those parents who resided in areas outside previously all-White districts, innovative schemes had to be thought of in order to beat the system. In Reservoir Hills, Clare Estate, Asherville and Overport parents had to rely upon others to find their children places in areas such as Westville, La Lucia, Umhlanga Rocks and Morningside. Unlike the Indian dominated suburbs, there were no squatter camps in these areas and no rapid influx of Africans coming in as residents who were buying off properties that were being sold by Whites. In crude terms, Indians considered such areas as "safe areas" and ideal to send their children for an education.

The will to find out about schools was dependent upon several issues within the households of school-going children. They included issues such as awareness of how to go about finding another school that is considered "more suitable", the financial situation of the household, the trust in previously all-Indian schools and the ideological leaning of the children's parents. Those parents who chose to send their children to previously all-White schools went about negotiating with someone they knew in order to gain entry for their children. Their tasks were relatively easy if they had paternal kin residing in the area they chose to school their children. In the cases where there were two brothers, the required documentation of property tax receipts, electricity and telephone bills did not pose a problem because the surnames were the same. But where married sisters, maternal kin or friends were involved the documentation was accompanied by a covering letter from a person resident in the area, vouching for such persons as being resident with them either as family or as tenants on their properties.

At least two of the households in Clare Estate, that are depicted in Table 6.2 had the resources to send their junior and senior primary school children to schools outside their suburbs. But they lacked the knowledge of how to go about enrolling them. The process that one of the interviewees followed was an interesting one, since inquiries began with neighbours, then friends and later kin. It started in October 1997 when they first heard about some neighbours sending their children to schools in Westville. Not realising that applications ought to have been made by July of that year, they briefly discussed it and only dismissively thought about the prospect of enrolling their children in Westville. They made their first inquiry through a neighbour who was already sending his children to the school in Westville, and were informed then that it was too late to enroll. In January 1998 they approached a friend who agreed to approach the principal to consider the children's enrolment. But the response was negative because all the classes were allegedly filled even before the year began. They later approached relatives for advice because they were raising their children's hopes and expectations of a new and "better school". He advised them that a school in La Lucia, which was twice the distance to that in Westville and had a fee requirement that was substantially higher, was the only option left. The relative approached the principal of the La Lucia school, who agreed to admit the children.

There was a very important ambiguity that emerged in the course of the conversations that took place with the interviewees. One of them, a teacher once remarked: *"I am sending both my children to White schools in Westville. But let me be honest, I don't think these schools are up to much. They can't match the standards in Indian schools. We do a much better job with our children. Their mathematics used to be far too low for our schools. And now, with all the changes taking place the syllabi are now the same. But the White teachers are not doing their jobs like us. I see it in the way my children are being taught."* This statement was made in the presence of her spouse, who agreed with her and who was also a teacher. Both taught in the Phoenix township for Indians and they had a high regard for the ex-House of Delegates schools. Their statements prompted the soliciting of more views on the differences between former Indian and White schools. Twelve out of the fifteen teachers, who were asked their opinion on the quality of education between these two schools, felt that the Indian schools and their Indian teachers were doing a better and harder job than their White counterparts. They believed that the former Indian schools performed better in the science subjects than the former White schools. From the 106 households that were sending their children to former White schools, 27 of them belonged to teachers who were still employed in the profession. The indicators that they used, rather than specific criteria, was the general overall performance in the former White schools, where Indian pupils were the bigger takers of scholarly awards. Most Indian pupils, it has been alleged, came from former Indian schools where they had a sound grounding. Their entry into White schools did not pose as severe problems to them as did the entry of African pupils into Indian schools. White pupils were seen to be competing against formidably taught Indian pupils, thereby raising the standard within White schools itself. The exit of such large numbers of pupils in turn created a perception of lower standards in Indian schools, brought about mainly through the attempts to teach African pupils through a second language medium *i.e.* English. But the teachers denied that standards have been lowered, rather the pace of work had been slowed down to enable African students to think and work in English. To most teachers, their pride in their professions was being questioned and they felt a need to defend it. Although Indian schools in most areas had already acquired a reputation for becoming Africanised, the issue of standards was still defended by most that remained in their schools as teachers.

Conclusion

In view of the information that has been presented above, certain fundamental questions ought to be raised about the ideological and racial leanings of people of Indian origin in South Africa. For instance, a decisive question that ought to be asked is: "Have the Indians acted purely out of racist sentiments in choosing to send their children to the former all-White schools instead of leaving them in the former Indian schools that were walking distances from their homes and which were not so financially taxing?" To attempt to answer this question in just one way or the other would be tantamount to oversimplification of an issue that is much more complex than otherwise. Those who have been identified as "Indians" for this project are also quite disparate in their linguistic backgrounds, religious practices, eating habits and other patterns of normative behaviour. Despite being lumped together as "Indians" issues such as religion, home language, food and associated taboos, caste and class backgrounds have much to do in the way pupils thinking is shaped both at home and in school. Their only commonality is their geographical origin.

In trying to answer the question that is posed above, the issue of the couple, noted above, who were teachers in the Indian township of Phoenix ought to be raised as well. Why is it that those two people who had such a high degree of pride in their profession and in the competence of Indian teachers in general, not enroll their children in either of the school that they taught, especially since these were Indian dominated schools? In this instance, as in the case of other teachers who sent their children to former White schools, surely class should take precedence over race. The teachers, by virtue of their professions, salaries and the areas in which they lived, fell squarely within the sphere of a middle-class status. Yet on the one hand they shifted their children away from their suburban schools because it was increasingly enrolling African pupils, while on the other hand they could not see it fit to take their children to the under-class Indian township in which they taught. The former issue sounds like a genuinely race inspired motive, while the latter issue sounds like a genuinely class inspired motive. Should it be one or the other, or can it be a mixture of both?

What parents were doing in these instances was actually communicating their class and ethnic differences. The inter-group contacts that they faced between African children in previously all-Indian schools and later with Whites in previously all-White schools induced a reorientation of their ethnic position. Many previously all-White schools have introduced the teaching of Indian languages, religious education and religious societies through parent requests. To this extent they articulated their differences with Whites. But what was clear in these situations was that they identified with the White population because of their history of literacy and a history of commitment to education of their offsprings. They failed to identify with the African population because they lacked the history of the extent of educational achievements that have been witnessed in the White or Indian communities over the past century. Although almost fifty years ago, there is a semblance of what this study reveals to work of Park (1950) and the Chicago School. Park, together with his associates in the 1920s and 1930s, was interested in the way in which ethnic groups remained distinctive in American cities, despite the 'melting pot' theory and the predictions of dissipation of ethnic exclusivity. They saw the city as a kind of ecological system, which had its own internal dynamic that allowed individuals, and groups to take advantage over certain opportunities and exercise constraints over others. This was because the city contained several distinct "social worlds" based on class and race or ethnicity. The social worlds in which each group lived, such as the tax paying residents and the squatters researched for this study, had its own distinctive physical neighbourhoods divided by their own historical experiences, access to resources and ethnic or racial differences. Indians pride themselves in having their origins entrenched in a literate civilisation and believe they have much to be proud about in South Africa for the ways in which they continued with the tradition of literacy and exploited the opportunities made available to them in education. Their association with White schools is, therefore, seen as an attempt to sustain this tradition, which was not as well developed in the African population.

REFERENCES

1. Dr. R. Rambiritch, "*A Brief Review of Indian Education*: 1860-1960".
2. The Natal Mercury, *Indian Educational Supplement*, Tuesday, September 28, 1965.
3. Somarsundaram Cooppan (1948) "A Summary of the Education of the Indian in Natal, 1860-1947".
4. The Natal Mercury, *Indian Education Supplement*, Tuesday, September 28, 1965.
5. *Ibid.*
6. *Sunday Tribune*, 16 June 1996 and 6 December 1998 respectively.
7. Independent on Saturday, 17 April 1999.

CHAPTER SEVEN

To Go or Not To Go: Increasing Thoughts about Emigration

Introduction

A new mood of emigration has set itself into motion and has gained momentum in a manner that has suggested more confusion than otherwise about emigration, particularly as it relates to normative expectations among Indians about living in one place and showing stability in thought and mind. For Indians, living a settled life and building upon the property that one acquires is generally a hallmark of achievement and success. In view of this statement and of what is to follow below, a quotation from the 1944 NIC Memorandum needs rehearsal here: "Due regard must be had to the character of the Indian which differs vastly from that of the European or the Native. The Indian, regardless of the size of his income will hardly ever fail to meet the instalments due on a property he is buying. He has an inborn urge to own his own home however humble, and he will endure amazing personal sacrifices to achieve this end" (Annexure B, p. 46). Much earlier, Sannyasi and Chaturvedi (1931: 28), writing on the experiences of indentured Indians, quoted a British colonial officer who was experiencing difficulty in acquiring Indian recruits for their colonies: "The first thing to which I would draw very careful attention is this: that Indians are a home loving people. They have not got the migratory instinct strong in their blood, like the British or the Irish. It would perhaps be true to say that Indians have less of the migratory habit taken as a whole, than the people of any other country as a whole." In support of this observation, Jain (1993: 4) has stated that the large scale emigration of Indians in modern times and their permanent settlement in other parts of the world is in a sense a surprising phenomenon. Historically, Indians were averse to crossing the 'black waters' *(kala pani)* because it was traditionally regarded as full of peril to the Hindu's soul. Apart from small trading communities, there was no large-scale settlement in new countries until the nineteenth century. According to Sharma (n.d) Indians were conned, coerced and cajoled into working as indentured labourers for the British. They were hardly willing to migrate to unknown lands.

But thoughts about migration among South African Indians have undergone radical change. Many have considered their continued existence in the country to be a risk to their personal and family safety. At least five countries have become popular destinations for South Africa's professionals and business people from the White, Coloured and Indian populations *viz*. Australia, New Zealand, United Kingdom, Canada and United States of America. A few odd responses from interviewees touched on India, Singapore and the Middle East, but not with the same conviction as those who were already in a state of preparedness to leave for any of the first group of countries. Their reference to the latter three countries was largely out of frustration with the level of helplessness that they felt in South Africa and the relative peace and methods of justice in them. India was an important comparison with South Africa because of its endemic poverty yet low levels of crime. It was in these areas of references that strong cultural comparison, ethnocentric and racially based statements were made, in addition to the nostalgia with which relative peace, and law and order were remembered under White minority rule in South Africa. The countries named above were especially favourable because they were English speaking and were of first world status. Their attraction lay in their political and economic stability, the opportunities in employment and for further development of their children.

Understanding the Motivation for Emigration

The issue of emigration was churned out of continuous and frequent reference to issues linked to important milestones in the political changes that began from the time of F. W. de Klerk's reign as president of South Africa. In order to understand the issue of emigration, there must be an analysis of responses from two important questions that were linked to the issue. They were:

- *"What are your views on the state of the nation before 1991 when the African dominated political organisations were unbanned, and after the 1994 general elections?*

- *For which political party did you vote in 1994 and for which one would you vote in 1999?*

The initial stages of this project did not focus on emigration at all. At least sixty of the interviews were carried out before this aspect was included in the interview schedule. By this stage it became apparent that the question ought to be asked. The negative responses that the last five preceding chapters have revealed are testimony to the waning confidence that interviewees have shown in South Africa's first stage of its post-apartheid history. At least forty-five respondents from among the first sixty interviewees had expressed the desire to emigrate, or who knew of others who were already in the process of doing so. Their reasons were common: high crime, poor police enforcement, rising costs of household security, deteriorating educational standards, a weak and overworked judiciary supported by a constitution that gave criminals the same rights as their victims, rising unemployment, affirmative action in favour of Africans—thereby marginalising Indians, the country's devaluing currency, and a shrinking economy. But the interviewees' views on wanting to leave South Africa were not consistently documented up to this stage.

On a national level the rapid increase in emigration received considerable attention soon after the 1994 general election. A survey by the Human Sciences Research Council (HSRC) early in 1998 showed that at least 74 per cent of South Africa's skilled labour force was considering emigrating.[1] The annual cost to the economy was calculated at R250 million rands, taking into account the costs of training and replacing skilled personnel and positions that were lying vacant. Since 1993 there was a skills shortage ranging from 8 per cent that rose to 51 per cent in October 1998. The HSRC's investigation into their respondents' perceptions of the economy found that 57 per cent thought the economy was going to worsen. As a result of this perception, an average of 800 highly skilled people per month were estimated to be leaving the country, totalling more than 10,000 per annum. Econometrix, a team comprising economic analysts, calculated that for every skilled person, at least 10 jobs are created for unskilled persons, translating into a loss of 100,000 unskilled jobs per annum when skilled people emigrate.

While a highly emotive debate prevails throughout the country about emigration, the test really lies in the government staving off a lapse into economic devastation, as witnessed in the performances of post-Independence African countries. But the state's response to this growing crisis was interesting. The first president of post-apartheid South Africa, Nelson Mandela, fuelled the debate by accusing those who have emigrated and who are thinking of doing so, as "cowards". He added: *"Go and good riddance.... The real South Africans are remaining in South Africa".* His Deputy President, Thabo Mbeki, reduced the growing tendency to emigrate to the "non-African" segments of the population who were opposed to the application of affirmative action policies. Mbeki's contribution was: *"My only response (to the threats) is that it is probably better that they leave"*[2]. But in this research the interviewees' reasons for wanting to emigrate were neither cowardly nor simplistically based on affirmative action. Their responses were often related to conditions prior to and after the 1994 general elections, with accounts of how they have been affected by stress and trauma through personal experiences.

Analysis of Responses to Questions on Emigration

At least one question was fundamental to ascertaining the feelings of respondents on emigration: "What are your views on the state of the nation before 1991 when the African dominated political organisations were unbanned and after the 1994 General Election?" A numerical analysis of the above question provided at least four categories of respondents. They could be divided into the following: positive, negative, ambivalent and apathetic. Each category had common types of responses that allowed them to be grouped together.

This question elicited information on at least four major issues *viz.*

- The levels of confidence and security they felt for their personal and family safety under White minority rule during apartheid and after April 1994.
- Their chances of either acquiring employment if they had to leave their current positions and of their children acquiring work on completion of their studies.
- Their opinions of the government's performance since the ANC takeover in 1994, especially in their policies and successes in education, employment, roads servicing and law and order.

- Their faith in the future of the country.

Interviewees were given an indication of these four aspects only when they prompted the specificity in their replies. Most of them had understood the question as entailing those issues and spoke freely about their feelings on them. It was often made explicit by them that they were happy to talk about the issues, especially if it could impact upon policy issues that would provide a safer and more secure future in the country. These kinds of responses came especially from those who spoke much about emigrating and who wanted to be convinced that there is a future for themselves and their children in the country—a point that will be discussed later.

Table 7.1 is an illustration of how many made up each category among the 255 interviewees.

Table 7.1: Illustrating four categories of responses from 255 interviewees on the question above

Responses	*Number*
Positive	51
Negative	142
Ambivalent	36
Apathetic	26
Total	**255**

It is clear from Table 7.1 that those who were distinctly positive about the period before and after the elections were a minority, while those who were firmly negative about transformation were in the majority. The issues that interviewees referred to as positive, constituted substantial changes that were a significant breakaway from the apartheid past. The positively minded were almost in unison in referring to the post-election trials and tribulations as a situation that is likely to be found in any emerging democracy such as South Africa's. At least seven of the 51 interviewees initially responded to the question with cynicism and dismissed any negativity about the future of the country with contempt. They saw such comments as coming only from people who are pessimists and as one stated: *"Only those who are racist and not willing to give a Black government the chance to restructure will not see any hope in the future of this country."* The positive changes that they have identified include:

- the repeal of the 1950 Group Areas Act as well as the 1950 Population Registration Act,
- freedom of movement—allowing people to live where they choose and associate with whom they please,
- freedom of speech,
- the country's integration into the global economy without the constraints of the past-during apartheid,
- the freedom to vote for a political party of one's choice,
- the right to send one's child to a school or tertiary institution that is nearest to one's home or any other school or tertiary institution if they can afford to do so, and
- greater degree of accountability and transparency in government offices—as witnessed by the number of people who are being publicly exposed through state action against corrupt officials.

These were the issues that the positively minded spoke about as reasons for encouragement in a future South Africa. The negative issues that the other categories identified were also spoken about to an extent by this category of interviewees, but almost always in a strong defensive way about the state and its problems. Their common view was that the problems were not so insurmountable that they could not be remedied. For these reasons they saw themselves as devout South Africans who had a positive outlook for the future of the country or with no intention of emigration.

The ambivalent and the apathetic were a variety of respondents who ranged from people who were highly conscientised, to others who displayed either virtual ignorance or disinterest in the political situation. From among those who were highly conscientised, their attitudes veered more towards apathy and disappointment in transformation than in a positive outlook. There was however two kinds of apathy *viz.* that which was generated by a totally negative attitude towards transformation and that which was generated by sheer disinterest in politics. The difference between the two was that the former group was more aware of political transformation and the latter showed little or no interest.

There was a distinctly different level of articulation among the under class residents in Phoenix and those who rented in outhouses in the middle-class suburbs, whose responses were generally, and understandably, of a simplistic nature. But their replies provided important insights into how they were conceptualisng and responding to change. They usually replied in terms of either the immediate benefits they acquired after the 1994 elections or the problems they experienced since then. Among this group of forty-five interviewees, there was a distinct mindset that could only articulate their aspirations in terms of what South Africa had to offer them. Their class status, demonstrated by their low levels of education and menial low paid jobs, restricted their thinking to their immediate needs and survival. There was a clear resignation among all of them that the fate of the country lay in powers beyond their understanding. While they were aware of the issues such as high crime rates, unemployment, and deteriorating schooling conditions, their responses were to remain employed, keep away from crime ridden areas and from public or isolated places after dusk and to send their children to the nearest school. At least three responses capture the level of interests within this group. A retrenched factory employee, who had just given birth to a child, made the first. The second statement was made by a sixty years old male who considered himself disabled and who had qualified for a disability grant in May 1995, and the third statement was made by a retrenched forty-seven old male:

- *"Before apartheid, it was difficult to get free treatment in the hospitals. Now it is different for us. I can take my baby until she is six years old and she will get free treatment."*
- *"For how long I was applying for a disability grant, but I never got it. Now with the new government after the election, I just got it—after more than three years of waiting."*
- *"Ya well, what must we do now. There's no more jobs, so we must just eat the crumbs that our families give us. All the money I had is almost finished now."*

One aspect that all of these forty-five interviewees had commonly stated was that crime was a major factor that was affecting their lives. At least eleven of this group had personally fallen victim to violent crime and gave lengthy accounts of how they were accosted and beaten. At the time of the interviews, a thirty-one old father of one child was still recovering from a severely beaten face that was a result of a mugging in Central Durban on a Friday afternoon in August 1998. He was confronted by three African youths who thought he had his weekend wages with him. He claimed that nobody dared to help him despite the fact that the streets were busy. Another housewife claimed that two African males accosted her while she was hanging clothes to dry outside at 10h00. She was beaten, though not severely, and taunted until she gave away the R600 (rands) that her husband had kept away for the rent that was to be paid that weekend. Thereafter she was bound and gagged and left in the room until her child returned from school at 12h45. It was the fourth incident in less than three weeks that occurred in an arbitrarily demarcated cluster of twelve houses that were targeted for interviews. Further information from the neighbours about the incident suggested that the woman was raped and was too traumatised to face the neighbours for at least two months. Her long absence from the neighbourhood and information that some of her closer and more intimate neighbours had gathered from her strongly suggested rape. But no such charges were laid and no arrests were made in any of the incidents that occurred in that immediate neighbourhood.

The reaction from the people in the area was to form a vigilante group—that was monitored by the police. Neighbourhood solidarity was shown through this formation. It had brought the residents, from more than the twelve houses that were targeted for interviews, closer together. Their targets were clearly defined—unknown Africans walking aimlessly in an area that was inhabited only by Indians and which was far away from any squatter camp and African township. Their reasons were based on their experiences that Africans were the culprits in the attacks that they witnessed. Herein lied the racially based perception that spawned the dichotomy of Indians as victims and Africans as perpetrators. A member of the vigilante group once remarked that they had the full backing of the police who claimed that they were constrained in following official procedure. The frustrations on the side of the residents and the police had led to a tacit agreement that if anyone was caught for burglary or stealing cars, then the vigilantes were at liberty to kill that person. The understanding was that criminals were easily released from prison and returned into civil society only to repeat the same crimes. Nobody was apprehended during the research period, although the crime rate was allegedly significantly reduced after the formation of the vigilante group.

While there were several convincing replies about the future of South Africa from the group of under-class interviewees, their most negative ideas emanated from the violence they personally experienced. It was a problem that they just had to keep away from, without much faith in the idea for instance, that mobilising against the state through some kind of unified action could at least send a symbolic message to the authorities to control violence.

To most of the middle and upper class interviewees, their mobilising and symbolic action against the problems that are rampant in South Africa, are seen through various kinds of action. A businessman's response captures the middle class's response to this: *"The vigilante groups in residential areas, the role of the press in exposing corruption in government and incompetent leaders, the slowing down of foreign investments, and the huge exodus of highly qualified people from the country, are messages enough for the government to catch a wake-up call. If they don't, what has happened in Kenya, Uganda, Zimbabwe and Mozambique, is going to happen here soon. They better realise that the conditions in many sectors during apartheid were not as bad as they are today. Everything that we thought was not going to happen in this country is already happening."* The starkest contrasts in the conditions before and after the 1994 general election came especially from educationalists and business people. Each category compared the relevant periods and remembered the conditions under which they worked with nostalgia. An important assessment emerged from analysis of the data in this category of respondents. With most having a more mature sense of awareness of change than the under-class group discussed above, two periods were mostly remembered with glee. The first was the release of Nelson Mandela and the unbanning of the ANC, as well as the other political organisations. This event was seen as a welcome culmination of the urban guerilla war that was being waged by the ANC against the apartheid regime. In this situation almost anybody could become a victim of the attacks, especially in crowded shopping complexes. The termination of urban attacks was associated with an immediate release of stress in the minds of most citizens. The second period was the last few weeks just prior to the election in April 1994. Most of the interviewees could recall the period with a high degree of hope for political and economic stability in South Africa. The same number felt that conditions rapidly deteriorated no more than a few months after the elections. The high frequency of car-jackings, followed by daylight burglaries and subsequently on cash-in-transit heists, among other forms of crime, was signs of rapid decay of the moral fibre of civil society.

In continuous harping upon such negative issues, the middle and upper class interviewees were also justifying their reasons for looking outside the country for peace of mind and more stable conditions under which they could survive. Most of them saw emigration as a solution to their anxieties and fears about the future. Their awareness of the political and economic problems in most of the countries in the African continent had reinforced a widely held stereotype that lay latent for a period just before the election and for a few months after the event. That latent feeling is that African governments are rightly associated with the inability to govern effectively, and with mismanagement, corruption and autocratic rule that eventually gives rise to political rebellion. The turmoil in a number of countries such as Burundi, Democratic Republic of Congo, Uganda, Mozambique, among others, had fuelled this growing lack of confidence that so many of the interviewees have expressed. A sample of ten short statements made by middle-class interviewees who were negative provide an indication of how they felt:

- "*First it was the rise of political violence which tore this province apart. Now that it is on the decline, the criminal element has taken over. Where will it stop?*"
- "*Before 1991, although there was racial segregation and apartheid, there was also a degree of control, especially on violence. Now freedom means freedom to commit crime, acts of violence, bribery, corruption, etc. There's no hope.*"
- "*Education and the finances of the country have gone from bad to worse. All you ever hear now-a-days about the government is corruption.*"
- "*Before 1991 there seemed to have been greater job security, financially most of us were better off. Education in certain areas was making greater headway. But you can't say the same anymore.*"
- "*The country is just going backwards. Although we were worried that this was going to happen at first, we were sure it would recover. But now you can see that it is just drifting away without any hint of recovery.*"
- "*Before 1991 we were sitting on a time bomb. After the 1994 elections we were going through the pains of building a united nation. We were all excited about it then. But up to now the government hasn't been able to get its act together.*"

- *"Before 1991, life was difficult during apartheid. After the 1994 election crime has made it worse. This country's violence is a slower form of torture for its citizens, but just as bad as Rwanda. The difference is that in Rwanda people were killed in larger numbers at one time. Here it is only that people are getting killed more slowly."*
- *"Before 1991 there were too many restrictions. After 1991, there is only a semblance of greater freedom. But the high crime rate has held back the progress we were hoping for. We've just come back from London, where people were really living their lives. The whole city is awake after dark. Over here everyone is forced to go to sleep soon after dark because of fear. Is this freedom?"*
- *"No doubt the state of the nation was better before 1991 and worse after the 1994 elections. We can't sleep with our windows open anymore in the summer, because you don't know who might just shoot at you any time. I doubt that it will get any better."*
- *"When a country's currency starts devaluing at the rate that ours is devaluing, it is clear that the country's economy is no longer in the hands of its own people. Foreign interests will just continue to knock our economy in the same way that they have done in other developing countries. The ANC has sold us out to the multinationals. And the Nats used to call them communists!"*

The atmosphere of gloom and doom had become so prevalent that it overshadowed the positive changes that had taken place in South Africa. Confidence in political leaders and their parties have reached an all time low. This situation has had a direct bearing on how people felt about the general election in 1999, which is discussed below.

Who did you vote for in 1994 and who will you vote for in 1999?

Information on this question was collected between June 1997 and February 1999. Since the political situation in South Africa is dynamic and ever changing, the information collected within this period could be inconsistent with the situation at the time of the election on 2 June 1999. For instance no information was gathered on the United

Democratic Movement (UDM) that was started in 1998 by two prominent politicians who rebelled against their parties, Roelf Meyer and Bantu Holomisa, who broke away from the National Party and African National Congress respectively. The UDM is a recent political formation that only acquired political party status in 1999 in order to participate in the general election.

There are two levels at which elections occur in South Africa during a general election *viz.* the national and provincial levels. At the national level thirteen political parties registered to participate, while in KwaZulu-Natal thirteen parties were registered. In order for a party to qualify for registration the requirement is to pay an amount of R100,000 and demonstrate the capacity to mobilise funds for sustainability. At the provincial level the requirement is a registration fee of R20,000 as well as the onus of having a support base to finance its activities. In order to qualify for seats in the National Assembly a political party ought to acquire at least 5 per cent of the national electoral votes, while 5 per cent of the provincial votes would earn a seat or seats, *pro rata*, at the provincial level.

Their experiences and perceptions of transformation in South Africa have determined the responses that interviewees have provided to voting. The negative attitudes that are illustrated in Table 7.1 had a direct impact on the responses to voting in 1999. The choices of political parties and the indecision of the interviewees have illustrated how voters were thinking about the 1999 elections. The information in the table is an indication of this.

The figures in Table 7.2 provide an indication of the uncertainties that transformation has produced. It is important to discuss the major political parties listed on Table 7.2 and the other responses that have been noted because of South Africa's peculiar history. Of special interest here is the ANC. Only 37 (18%) of those interviewed were emphatic about supporting the party. Their history in the struggle against apartheid was not always understood nor was it frequently mentioned. In reference to it, the respondents tended to separate the personality of Nelson Mandela from the rest of the organisation. He was widely looked at as a trusted, strong and influential figure that contributed much to the political stability of the country. For this reason people adored him and expressed a desire to see him continue in his contributions to political stability after he retired from political office. Odd cynical remarks were made against him in a few interviews—the strongest being: *"You can't expect a prisoner who stayed in jail for twenty-seven years to suddenly rule the country."*

Table 7.2: Illustrating the pattern of voting in 1994 and the possible choices in 1999 from 195 interviewees

Political choice	*Number—1999*	*Number—1994*
ANC	37	57
New National Party	21	68
Democratic Party	6	11
Inkatha Freedom Party	1	0
Confidential	2	2
Will not/did not vote at all	5	-
An Indian party/Minority Front	3	52
A White party	5	-
Undecided	96	-
Total	**195**	**188 *7 claimed not to have voted = 195**

But the rest of the ANC was not looked at favourably by the majority of the interviewees. They justified their views against the party's leadership by referring to what is now understood as endemic corruption and mismanagement. The state of education, health and justice were continuously referred to and blamed on the ANC. A striking note from the more conscientised and alert middle class respondents, was the expressed understanding that there would be economic instability for a period after the 1994 election, as a result of the ANC's inexperience in government. But there was a sense of deep shock and disappointment in the failure to create employment and bring about at least a semblance of a safe and secure environment that was congenial to developing a better sense of loyalty and patriotism.

From the nine categories after the first in Table 7.2, at least twenty-three interviewees made an emphatic statement that they *"will definitely not vote for the ANC"*. Six of the twenty-three had voted for the ANC in the 1994 election, of which five voted both nationally and provincially and one voted for it only nationally, but voted for the Minority Front in the province. The succession to President Nelson Mandela's office was of particular concern among many respondents. In four group interviews with a total of twenty-seven people and in forty-three interview schedules serious concern was expressed about the ability of Thabo Mbeki to sustain the racial and ethnic stability that Mandela was able to procure. Mbeki's association with controversial but high profile individuals such as Winnie Mandela and Peter Mokaba—widely viewed by many as eccentric people—who are on public record making racist statements especially against Whites, have cast doubt about the ability of the ANC to maintain a non-racial ideology that made them likeable during the euphoria of the 1994 election.

The situation with the other parties is that the National Party (registered as the New National Party for the 1999 election—joined in early 2000 by the Democratic Party to form the Democratic Alliance) and the Minority Front (targeting mainly the Indian population) had lost substantial support—at least from among the interviewees. This trend is consistent with national polls that have been carried out on the likely performance of the political parties. Only one person vouched for the Inkatha Freedom Party, while six stated that they would vote for the Democratic Party. While this indicates that they too have lost support, the situation during the election is likely to change for the Democratic Party. There appeared to have been a significant rise in popularity for the party among people of Indian origin. The party's aggressive campaign for the 1999 election since the beginning of the year appeared to have paid off with some minority groups. They took up minority issues, and particularly in KwaZulu-Natal, campaigned on Indian fears and concerns around education issues and affirmative action. In several gatherings during the months of April and May 1999, that were not intended to collate research data, there has been talk of supporting the party for a number of reasons, such as:

- "*The National Party is finished and they are still too racist. We'll have to vote for the DP.*"
- "*The IFP will lose badly in the next election, and the ANC is sure to take over.*"
- "*We must teach the ANC a lesson and vote for the DP.*"
- "*ANC rule has proved that the Black man stands for chaos. The DP is our only hope now. You can't beat White rule. Under them we had order and safety.*"
- "*There isn't anyone else to trust in. Maybe the DP could make a difference.*"

It is significant that the biggest number among the categories listed on Table 7.2 is the undecided. Within this group the question about which party to vote for in the 1999 election often ignited reactions to at least one of three issues *viz.*

1. turmoil, uncertainty, and violence in the country;
2. vitriolic attacks against the ANC for its poor leadership; and
3 no trust in politicians.

On several occasions the media recorded what they viewed as apathy in the Indian population for showing a serious enough interest in registering to vote. The requirement to vote in the 1999 election was to first register formally with a computerised bar-coded identity book. In most of the predominantly Indian suburbs such registration did not take place on the scale that was expected, despite the fact that the registration dates were extended several times. It was especially from this group that the urge to emigrate was expressed. Their apathy was entrenched in a situation of almost total loss of confidence in the country's future and they could only see hope for themselves through emigration.

Emigration—Not an Individual Choice

There were three categories of people who could be included under the caption of emigration. There were those who:

- already qualified for residence in a foreign country and were preparing to leave,
- were seriously considering emigrating and were in the process of inquiring about foreign residency,
- wished they could emigrate but were refraining from doing so because of financial constraints and the fear of restarting their lives at the risk of failure, and
- considered themselves too old to emigrate but were either encouraging or not stopping their children if they wished to do so.

The last two groups constituted the majority of the 195 interviewees.

Although the majority of those who wanted to emigrate were from amongst the group who were undecided voters, there were also those who were from the households of interviewees who strongly supported the ANC and believed in the future of the country. Such households were ideologically split about the capacity of the ANC to govern and to generate confidence within the population about the viability of the country's future. In at least two interviews the nature of the conversation about political transformation and emigration evoked inputs from other family members about the interviewees perceptions. Such family members were not inclined towards the ANC and very receptive towards talk of emigration. In both households the interviewees were strong-minded men and household heads who were avid ANC supporters. Their control over their families' decisions was evident by virtue of them remaining as South African citizens. In one case, a housewife married to a factory owner felt that Canada would be the country to emigrate, since she once lived there with family. Her preference was immediate emigration. But her spouse's reply was: *"Tell me what is in Canada that you will not find here?"* The husband's reply was also determined by his retired parents' refusal to emigrate. Their dependence on him made this an uncompromising decision with him. In the second instance, the wife, a physiotherapist, felt inclined and stated that she was comfortable to go along with her husband's (a chartered accountant) decision to remain in South Africa. It was their children's decision to consider emigrating, but who could not because their father objected. One was a tertiary institution lecturer and the other was a graduate in business economics who was unemployed for almost a year since completion of her studies. Both differed strongly with their father on his views in the future of South Africa and were adamant that emigration was the answer to their problem[3].

It became apparent from twenty-five cases that were closely monitored and revisited—for whom emigration was eminent—that the decision was not always a matter of personal choice. It depended on several factors, the most common of which was the settlement of relatives overseas who could facilitate an easy adaptation to their new environments. Respondents often voiced their concern about how the extended family—particularly the elders—felt about emigration, especially since many were not in good health. Their anxiety tended to revolve around the impact their departure will have on family unity—especially in cases where entrenched business interests were involved. Its control, care, distribution and sharing of family wealth, were impediments to their final decisions. Where the older generation were unable to tend to family businesses, the decision to emigrate was even more problematic. But for those who had the bare minimum to take away, the resources to return to South Africa frequently enough posed a problem. The issue here was not to burden elderly folk with their concern about the health and conditions under which the incumbents live there. Hence, the costs to return and visit family frequently enough added its own burden. Continuing with religious practices was also a factor in the decision to emigrate. In the process of arranging their final emigration, proximity to religious institutions *i.e.* especially Hindu or Muslim Centres of worship was also given serious consideration. However, in cases where the mood to emigrate was positive, there appeared to be an expectation to create conditions for more family and friends to join them.

There was a distinct process that was rooted in the kinship ties of the individuals who decided to emigrate. While the decisions were made between spouses, they first had to discuss it with both sets of parents and extended families with utmost sensitivity. In most instances the elderly folk initially objected to the decisions but also showed understanding. In at least one case the death of two elderly people was attributed to the emigration children, as the case below illustrates.

> *In 1997 S.T. then a thirty-five-years-old bank employee, emigrated to San Diego, North America, to co-own a motel with a relative. His parents, "happy" that their youngest son emigrated, visited him in December 1997. Soon after they returned in February 1998, his father had a severe heart attack and suffered a stroke while in hospital. He died two weeks later. In September 1998, S.T.'s wife's parents went to visit them in San Diego. His father-in-law suffered a heart attack and died a few days later. Since the costs of transporting deceased people are enormous the funeral had to take place in San Diego, while the family in South Africa observed the rituals in their respective houses.*

There was agreement on at least three issues that gave rise to people wanting to emigrate: the future for their children looked bleak, violence and the on-going prospect of the ANC remaining in power for a very long time. Although a seventy-two years old Gujarati businessman with all four daughters living overseas, once remarked: *"This country is going down so fast, that I have told my children not to remain here a minute longer if they could get out now. Three of them have done just that already.*[4] *I tell you too, get out now if you can—you should have gone yesterday. I had relatives in Uganda and Tanzania and I saw what happened to them there. But don't go to the U.S.A., they are the worst barbarians. Everyone carries guns there!"*

Four of the twenty-five interviewees who were closely monitored had left South Africa by March 1999. Two went to Australia, one to New Zealand and one to England. In all four cases there were families that encouraged them to make their choice. The convenience in this kind of arrangement was that the emigrants had immediate access to shelter, food and schooling for their children, which was pre-arranged by relatives or friends. Employment was also facilitated through other local networks of South African immigrants overseas or by the hosts themselves. Networking was an important mechanism for those either already emigrated or who were on the verge of doing so. This helped in reducing the isolation that emigrants are likely to experience in any such situation. In all four cases they were professionals, three of whom claimed to have acquired employment before leaving. News from the family of the fourth person was that both husband and wife acquired employment only weeks after landing (in New Zealand). The remainder of the twenty-five households was still in the process of finalising their emigration documents.

Most of those who were contemplating emigration but were unable to do so because of their weak financial standing, decided to encourage their children into professions that would facilitate easy access into one of the developed countries. They were one of two mindsets *i.e.* either emigrate with their children on the strength of their qualifications, or equip their children suitably until they are ready for employment and encourage them to leave the country while they remain behind. Most of the respondents from this group of interviewees have resigned their fate to South Africa, but they did not see much hope for their children. At least three of this group were between thirty and thirty-five years old, yet considered themselves too old to restart their lives in another country. Their common view was that they would be able to, as one succinctly put it *"...ride the storm until the end of our lives.*

But our children are unlikely to be able to. That's why we must encourage them to go. Lawlessness and affirmative action is what is going to be around here for a long time to come."

Such individuals actually fell within the range of lower middle-class and middle-middle class statuses. They had their homes with mortgage bonds that were manageable, wives and children who were also employed, and relatively good professions that could have acquired for them employment in one of the first world countries. But the discouraging factor to them was the lower return for their money if converted into one of the major international currencies. The devalued rand against currencies such as the British sterling and North American dollar has been the biggest deterrent for many whose dream it is to leave the country because of the range of problems associated with the nature of post-apartheid transformation. It is a dream that many have hoped will materialise for the sake of their children's future. They have entrenched in their minds the thought that as an Indian minority they will not be able to compete on equal terms either with Africans or Whites in the employment sector. Despite the crime rate being exceedingly high in the African townships, many were of the impression that the high rate of crime in their suburbs is a conspiracy against Indians emanating from the White and African populations. This they believe is evident in the number of squatter camps that are in predominantly Indian suburbs, and the crime that emanate from them—with Indians being the major victims.

In addition, the "sandwich theory", which is often used to describe the difficult circumstances that Indians believe is apt to describe their minority status, has been widely referred to. Many interviewees have continued to refer to the problems of Indians acquiring work by recalling the difficulties during apartheid and the problems in post-apartheid South Africa. The often-quoted phrase is: *"We were too Black during apartheid and not Black enough after apartheid."* The inference here is that Indians are sandwiched between a still economically powerful White elite and a numerically large, politically powerful African elite. The conspiracy theory against them, as many believe, was that White employers were deliberately and selectively applying affirmative action in favour of Africans as a ploy to divide the two racial groups. But a difficulty emerged with the interviewees when their attention was drawn to the public sector and their selective employment of Africans against more appropriately qualified Coloureds and Indians. Both the private and public sectors were acting against the spirit of the Labour Relations

Act that was promulgated in 1997. This is despite the Act's explicit wording that defines "Black" as all those who were previously not classified as "White", meaning the term should be all inclusive for Africans, Coloureds and Indians. For these reasons the interviewees have grown despondent about African majority rule and are, therefore, inclined to either excel in their studies or do the currently popular courses such as computer science and other science based qualifications in order to avoid unemployment or make it easier for their emigration. However, it will still be a costly affair for some and a mere dream to others as Desai's (1999: 81) observations reaffirms: *"Those who are not part of the political class or are not wealthy do not have the luxury of being temporary sojourners in foreign lands. For the middle class who wish to test the waters overseas, the only option is to accumulate capital by selling up to finance their trip. The lower classes, of course, cannot even emigrate to the next province."*

Conclusion

The widespread urge to emigrate is predicated upon the perceptions of the ineffectiveness of the ANC government and concerns about further deterioration in the spheres of education, health care, employment possibilities and security. If the HSRC survey that indicated that more than 70 per cent of the country's skilled labour force are considering emigration is correct, then the responses from the then President and Deputy President were serious miscalculations that are bound to cost the country dearly within the next few years. While there is certainly a situation of negative perception about African majority rule, it would be naive to reduce emigration to mere racist attitudes to those who wish to leave the country. The period leading up to the 1994 election and the very high and optimistic opinion that most respondents had for Nelson Mandela is an indication of the interviewees recognising and bestowing praise upon those who deserve it, irrespective of race. The concerns that they had over the President elect, Thabo Mbeki, are legitimate to the extent that such high profile leaders should not engage in racially loaded rhetoric on public platforms, even if it were their honest feelings. Such individuals have a much larger role to play in a country and continent that has come close to ruin through ethnic, racial and political differences. Indications from the sample for this study are consistent with the HSRC's survey. Although most who have past the age of thirty did not feel inclined to emigrate, they were certainly preparing their children to do so. If such a scenario does translate into reality, then more than a brain drain will affect the country. Unlike the conditions prior to the dismantling of apartheid, which was actually blamed for the initial stages of the brain drain, the reasons for this perennial migration are different. This time they are rooted in the "freedom movement's" inability to effectively control crime, to minimise the pain that other racial groups feel in their search for employment, and to create an environment that is congenial to stimulating political, economic and social development. The country's infrastructure is too complex and sophisticated to ignore the warning signs of the effects of massive emigration of skilled and professional labour.

REFERENCES

1. Reported in the *Independent on Saturday*, 1 October 1998.
2. *Sunday Tribune*, 14 June 1998.
3. Three months after the second interview with the family, the son acquired a job as a lecturer in English in South Korea.
4. His youngest daughter, a Charterred Accountant, emigrated to Canada six months later.

CHAPTER EIGHT

CONCLUSION

It was noted earlier that South Africa's transition to democracy was greeted with a euphoria that pleasantly surprised the world and perhaps even the very people who voted for democracy. Transformation was initially viewed with a sense of utopia that momentarily ignored the realities of the mammoth task ahead of the democratically elected government for social service delivery. Among Indians there was hope that democracy would usher in new avenues of political and economic opportunities for them, especially since they were an integral part of the 'Black disadvantaged masses' during the days of the struggle for emancipation. But their experiences of crime and its lack of containment have contributed directly to the swift erosion of confidence in the future of the state. Rising levels of land invasion by squatters and the resultant tension between Africans and Indians, deteriorating education and transport systems and thoughts about emigration, have radically turned around the utopia of April 1994 and generated largely negative perceptions in the way the state is handling these issues. Class cleavages are fast deteriorating into race-based cleavages that will eventually deliver a severe blow to attempts to create a society in which people do not premise their relationships with one another on race first. But even where Indians did not fall within the boundaries of middle-class, most of them also tended to articulate their perceptions about change with a siege mentality. Like their middle-class counterparts, they felt that there was growing tendency by Africans to overcrowd them and dominate. They often expressed a sense of helplessness because of their status as an ethnic minority. In each of the preceding chapters the ethnography has demonstrated how Indians are actually developing a consciousness of victimisation, accompanied by increasing anxiety about their future existence in South Africa. This is one of the reasons why so many, particularly from the middle class, have either emigrated, were contemplating emigration, or were preparing their children for a life in one of the first world countries.

Many of the fears among Indians are reinforced by the growing recurrence, as Filatova (1997) observed, about objections that there were too many Indians in high profile government positions and only selective treatment that Africans were allegedly receiving for civil service positions. Although the reality in South Africa since ANC rule is that the concept "Blacks" no longer applied to the collective reference to Africans, Indians and Coloureds as previously disadvantaged groups, especially in the application of affirmative action policies. It has become acceptable that affirmative posts imply that Africans be given preference over Coloureds and Indians—despite the national policy on affirmative action that all groups be treated equally. The on-going tension, between residents and squatters, bus owners and taxi operators, between pupils and teachers in schools, and the on-going assessment the future of civil life in South Africa and the growing tendency to emigrate, has contributed towards increasing negativity. Each time a violent or anti-social incident occurred between Indians and Africans, responses were almost invariably articulated in terms of ethnic or racial differences. Such responses increase the possibility of engulfing the two groups in more violent confrontations, which already occurred in 1949 and 1985 (Singh, 1992). For instance, an incident raised in chapter four about Indo-African relations after the stabbing to death of an African man, produced a potential situation for a serious clash. This was being fuelled by the growing schism between Indian residents and African squatters, Indian bus owners and African taxi operators, Indian and African school pupils, among other issues. While the clashes were largely along class lines, they were also being racialised, with interviewees often referring to violent robberies committed by Africans and the chaotic state of politics in post-Independence Africa.

The rising tensions between Africans and Indians have undoubtedly given rise to a fragile socio-economic situation between the two groups. But localised situations of fragile socio-economic conditions are often a reflection of the fragility of government at a national level. Such circumstances have led to many a coup in the African continent. Although the two fragile situations are not directly linked, up to March 2001 the possibility of a coup in South Africa appeared remote, the rumblings from the month of April at the highest level of government are beginning to show signs of such a possibility. The problems in the ANC could also be reduced to factions belonging to particular "tribal" affiliations. For instance, the accusations from the pro-Mbeki supporters (Xhosa) were actually against people from a range of other ethnic groups, particularly Pedi and Zulu. It is a known fact that leadership in the ANC has always been Xhosa dominated and is, therefore, likely to be the prime reason for challenges to it over time.

The ethnographic information has also illustrated how two important areas of historical significance to Indians *viz.* education and transport, have become increasingly restricted since the April 1994 elections. The uncertainty in education, brought about by massive cuts in subsidies, premature retirement of the most experienced teachers and administrative staff, and redeployment at the cost of family stability, has led to an all time low in the future of education in South Africa. There is a widespread perception that they are being eliminated from the teaching fraternity on ethnic lines, to be replaced in schools by African teachers and administrative staff. In the transport industry, the information has shown how Indian service providers are being systematically attacked or removed by African taxi operators who are trying to find a niche for their entrepreneurial ventures. This has taken place at a cost of a number of lives and the loss of livelihoods that have taken decades to consolidate. Indian transport providers have become vulnerable targets in a situation where their services often cater for African commuters.

The post-election experiences in areas such as in education and transport has contributed towards a feeling of increasing alienation in a climate of African empowerment. These feelings have become the prime reason for many to emigrate, to prepare for this event, or dream about it. It is once again a response to perceptions of unacceptable forms of either ethnically based hegemony exercised through state domination. Hirschmann (1970) argued that minorities may respond to state domination in one of three principal ways *i.e.* exit, voice or loyalty. Most of the respondents in the ethnographic information here have shown a tendency to 'exit', by continuously referring to emigration. Their voices, as many believe, are marginalised and their loyalty is restricted more to their families and kinship obligations than to the state.

The allegiance of Indians to South Africa is often seen in their loyalties to international sporting events. For instance, in 1999, the editor of the *Sunday Tribune Herald* (23 May 1999), which is a supplement to the Sunday Tribune that circulates this attachment mainly in Indian areas, accused Indians of being unpatriotic for not supporting the South African cricket team in the world cup, hosted in England. He alleged that most people of Indian origin supported one of the three other countries *viz.* India, Pakistan or Sri Lanka, because the South African team was mainly White, with just one player who was Coloured. The editor concluded by adding an element of subtle racism to his claim that Indians lacked patriotism. Two days later, the *Daily News* (25 May 1999) carried a headline about Indian attitudes towards the 2 June 1999 election: *"Indian voters reject black political parties"*. The article reported that 38 per cent of Indian voters had no faith in any political leader in the country, 33 per cent would vote for the New National Party (NNP), 15 per cent would vote for the Democratic Party (DP), while only 6 per cent and 1 per cent would vote for the ANC and IFP respectively. Clearly, the White dominated parties of the NNP and DP, according to the survey, enjoyed more political support among Indians. It quoted a prominent Indian political activist, as responding in the following words: "Indians have aspired to 'whiteness' and still do", but in an almost neutral manner immediately after this statement, he tried to contextualise the Indian response to the elections. He referred to the successful implementation over the decades, which resulted, he believed, in the Indian community becoming narcissistic and focusing on their own needs in isolation of the broader needs of society. Yet in 1984 when the then President of South Africa, P.W. Botha, had tried instituting a tri-cameral parliamentary system that created separate Houses for Whites, Coloureds and Indians, with each getting its support from their respective constituencies and dealing with their own affairs, the Indian population largely responded to the calls to boycott these race based elections. The respective politician then praised the Indians for ignoring the elections.

A fundamental question in such contradictory situations is: *"How do we make sense of an ethnic minority who refused to vote in the race based elections in 1984, refuses to support a Whites only team in international competition, and yet supports White dominated political parties in general elections?"* The answer to this question cannot be produced in a dismissive single sentence. Each of the situations require a contextual understanding that is likely to go beyond mere ethnocentricism, and certainly beyond the borders of the country. An interviewee's comment during fieldwork somewhat captures a widespread feeling to this question: *"Well, at least during White rule the crumbs that they threw for us was enough for us to build our lives. Now, you don't even get the crumbs...All over Africa there's starvation, coup d'etats, no proper planning, always no money, and always fighting...* ". Indian perceptions of and responses to transformation are indeed rooted in these kinds of understandings of politics in Africa. The comments by the editor of the *Sunday Tribune* and the prominent political activist are too simplistic, selective and devoid of understanding how the personal experiences of individuals collectively gathers momentum and filters into the wider population—shaping and determining their perceptions and responses. However, there is more to understanding this position among most Indians than their personal experiences.

There are three issues that ought to be brought to the fore in contextualising these largely negative attitudes *viz*. the history of marginalisation during White domination and its apparent continuation in the post-apartheid era, views on the successes and failures of the state, and the perceptions of politics in the continent of Africa in international perspective. The euphoria that has been described about the pre-election and immediate post-election period of April 1994 was an indication of the extent to which Indians, among the other racial categories, were looking forward to positive changes that were expected to embrace all South Africans without regard to race. But not too long after, affirmative action, applied mainly in favour of Africans, saw Indians, as well as Whites and Coloureds, being increasingly alienated from employment opportunities. The rising levels of crime, squatters and land invasion in mainly Indian areas in Durban and around Durban, racial quotas restricting the number of Indian students to medical school in KwaZulu-Natal favouring lesser qualified African students over better qualified Indian students, among a range of other problems, have had a major impact on the perceptions of and responses to transformation in post-apartheid South Africa. The state has not been blameless in this situation. A number of very poor performances by African personnel in areas such as education, health, housing, and rising unemployment have been understood as failures on the part of the government. In addition, continuous leadership crises have bolstered the situation. At least five of the Premiers in the nine provinces have been replaced within four years of the April 1994 election. In KwaZulu-Natal this most senior political office was changed three times. The month of April 2001 saw this situation extend itself to the office of the State President, while the political situation in Zimbabwe reached another crisis level. When these factors are added to the continuous allegations of corruption, incompetence in government offices, the fragility of leaders in high office, and ethnic and political violence elsewhere in Africa, it reinforces the fears of chaos and the erosion of the structures of civil society under African leadership. It is in this context that Indians tend to see White rule as representing stability and prosperity, and African rule representing the opposite. Arising out of this, Keith Richburg (1997), the African American journalist for the *Washington Post*, commented from personal experience, in his prelude to a critique on Africa:

> "*Maybe I should have just written a book on Africa that would have talked broadly about the politics, the possibilities, the prospects for change. But I'm tired of lying. And I'm tired of all the ignorance and hypocrisy and the double standards I hear and read about Africa, much of it from people who've never been there, let alone spent three years walking around amid the corpses. Talk to me about Africa and my black roots and my kinship about my African brothers and I'll throw it back on your face, and then I'll rub your nose in the images of the rotting flesh*"

The quotation above begs for introspection into a fundamental question: "What are the prime causes of violence in Africa and what does this mean for us in South Africa?" Very often the problem is with manipulation of tribal and ethnic sentiments, and academic literature abounds with such lessons from the past. Horowitz (1991: 86) has pointed out that in Nigeria, although the Hausa comprised 30 per cent of the population, and the Ibo and Yoruba 16 per cent and 17 per cent each, all three were major actors in the ethnic politics of the country, which in the first republic produced a Hausa-Ibo showdown. Richburg's (1997) illustration of how tribalism in Africa often manifests itself in the most violent ways to impose boundaries between tribal factions to keep politicians in office, is a variation of how ethnic sentimentality masquerades as a uniting factor in national politics, but is in fact a divisive force. For instance, in Kenya, while the late President Jomo Kenyata ingeniously used his Kikuyu loyalists to entrench his power, his successor, Daniel Arap Moi placed mainly his Kilenjin tribesmen in key government posts to consolidate his power. President Moi was ruthless towards his perceived enemies from within government circles, and slowly purged his rivals and critics from office. This process paved the way for a constitutional amendment enshrining his ruling Kenyan

African National Union as the sole legal political party. Thorold's (1997) description of Sufism and Yao identity in Southern Malawi provides a variation of how Malawi's first free democratic election in 1994 presented an opportune moment for the country's different ethnic groups to show their solidarity through their voting patterns. While Banda ruthlessly contained tribal dissension during his rule, he placed priority on the development of his Chewa tribe. This strengthened the suspicions over Banda and his Chewa tribe, leading most people from other groups to vote for their representatives from their own tribal groups. The result was that the Yao voted for their leader Muluzi, the Chewa for Banda and the Tumbuka for Chihana, while the other tribal groups voted against Banda and for whichever of the other two was nearest in proximity to them. In another demonstration of tribal solidarity in Cameroon, Nkwi (1997) demonstrates how the middle and upper class Kom ethnic representatives met in Yaounde the capital, in 1984, to establish an organisation to assist local communities to mitigate the effects of government neglect. They established the Njinikom Area Development Association (NADA) to provide hope and leadership and the services the state and local council were unable to provide in their region. Throughout its successes and failures, the mobilising and binding factor was clearly Kom ethnic solidarity.

Ethnic strife in Europe too has presented challenges for the political leadership in the continent. The on-going strife in Northern Ireland between Catholics and Protestants between 1969 and 1992 led to the death of more than three thousand people and to many more being injured. The Irish Republican Army and other nationalist paramilitaries have killed more than eight hundred members of the security forces and as many civilians (Hadden, 1994: 28). The end of the Cold War and the dissolution of the Soviet Empire, followed by the break up of the Soviet Union, Yugoslavia and Czechoslovakia, resulting in a central and eastern Europe of twenty-eight states. Only six of these states are considered homogeneous—Albania, Armenia, Czech Republic, Hungary, Poland and Slovenia. All of the remaining twenty-two states have national minorities comprising over ten per cent of the population. One of the most serious problems that have emerged thereafter was the rise of ethnic nationalism and the issue of minority rights. In view of this Miall (1994: 1) rightly points out:

> *"The appeal to ethnic nationalism, however, threatens to exclude minorities and encourages counter-nationalism...demands for*

self-determination may lead minorities to attempt to secede from the host state and create a state of their own."

The recent genocide in former Yugoslavia and the internecine wars between Serbians, Croatians, Muslims and ethnic Albanians have produced a sad reminder of the power and emotionalism associated with the assertion of ethnic identities.

People's common geographical origins, shared dialects, languages and customs, subservience to a single political authority and political structures, and a single religious background, were the real issues that bound them together and produced a common identity. They were not the imagined communities of a fictitious past and mythological origin that engendered a common solidarity. To suggest otherwise, as protagonists of Anderson's concept of "imagined communities" would concur, is actually to deny such realities. There are also those who subscribe to the view that imagined communities are not invented communities. However, the two are not mutually exclusive and different in meaning from each other. To imagine a community is to create if not to invent one in "as if" terms and not necessarily always in actual terms. The murder, maiming and widespread destruction of settled lifestyles in central and eastern Europe are not imaginary by any means, but real. Neither should these atrocities be understood as subtly coerced class wars that begin by remotely placed political elites only, although such people often have vested interests in stoking the flames of such battles. Ethnic identity is a deep-seated sense of self and community identity that often begin from a common geographical origin which is the seat of a common social system and language, out of which in-group and out-group identities emerge. Such identities may have a sense of strong symbolic continuity when transferred by such people through migration.

It is on the basis of these realities that political leaders in Europe have initiated the formation of what is presently being referred to as a transnational regime for minority rights. Although still relatively weak, the regime attempts to offer minorities protections under international law and international conventions such as the European Convention on Political Rights, and the political commitments entered into by member-states of the Conference on Security and Cooperation in Europe (CSCE). Attempts to achieve effectiveness of these initiatives are couched in at least three terms of requirements:

(1) States are encouraged to comply by making observance of

CSCE commitments a condition of participation in European institutions; (2) CSCE member-states have accepted a mutual right of monitoring compliance with the set standards; and (3) The CSCE is entitled to send fact finding and preventive diplomacy missions to their territories (Miall, 1994: 3).

It is indeed ironic that in a part of the world where the maturity of capitalism was enhanced by a strong culture of individualism (Western Europe), and where elitism and group identity was to be replaced by socialist cooperative behaviour (Eastern Europe), the first tangible signs of recognition of ethnic identities and group rights are now taking shape. Minority rights are defined as the rights of minorities to receive equal treatment, to practice their culture, religion and language, and to participate fully in the political and economic life of the state (Miall, 1994: 2). The recent ethnic clashes around the world are in essence a denial of these rights and have, therefore, enticed a proactive stance from many European governments against abuse of ethnic and minority rights. This is a significant shift away from the culture of human rights—that placed emphasis on individual rights, to a movement towards group rights. A transnational regime on minority rights will hopefully serve as a vehicle to conscientise entire populations, including narrowly minded fundamentalists or expedient and ruthless politicians in a way that will make ethnic differences more acceptable in a divided and turbulent world. But its effectiveness must not be overstated. While showing support for the idea, Mayall (1994) cautions that their distinctiveness from other parts of the world, in terms of capacity to protect, should not be exaggerated. He focussed on three issues that could offer minorities an assurance that their interests could be protected:

- develop of an additional layer of governance at European level, linked to stronger regions;
- a system of multilateral surveillance to monitor abuses; and
- an international capability to intervene to prevent massive abuses of human rights.

These points are like good omens when viewed against the 1999 intervention by NATO forces in Serbia to protect the ethnic Albanians from Serbian atrocities, or the pressures that European leaders put on the Austrian political structures when a right-wing fascist was elected as leader. At least in Europe, a precedent has been set to warn other chauvinistic leaders who thrive on ethnic dissent not to threaten the stability of the continent and world peace through such actions.

The atrocities and genocide in Africa, central and eastern Europe brings Peter Vale's ominous warning to stark reality: "We ignore ethnicity at our peril—if our society fails to engage it, it may rise to engulf us." (quoted in Howe, 1993). South Africa's surprisingly relatively peaceful transition to democracy in April 1994 created a euphoria that understandably shocked the nation and the world. The ANC's careful strategising and containment of ethnically based political forces, such as amongst Afrikaners and Zulus, helped to steer the country into an era of peace and hope. Much had depended upon the charismatic and persuasive leadership of the country's first President, Nelson Mandela. Mandela's route of reconciliation and an admirable avoidance of building a cult of personality worship around his twenty-seven years of incarceration turned the nation's attention away from avenging wrongs of the past. Yet it would not be entirely wrong to suggest that it is in Mandela's personality and his personal sacrifices against apartheid that the greatest respect was accorded, not in the organisation from which he came. The rumblings against his successor, President Thabo Mbeki, in April 2001, bears testimony to this. On the contrary, President Milosevec for instance, from former Yugoslavia, masqueraded as a magnanimous communist who worked closely with General Tito to manage their ethnically diverse country. But his genocidal actions against the ethnic Albanians showed no sign of a committed socialist. The breakdown of the Berlin Wall and the dismantling of the Soviet Union gave rise to a rapid surge of free market principles into Yugoslavia, and caught its leadership unaware. There was no time and inadequate preparation for a reorientation in the country to meet the challenges of an overpowering new ideology that brought socialism to an abrupt halt. The political leaders in Yugoslavia, such as Milosevic, resorted to expedient tactics by exploiting the suppressed ethnic grievances that were not allowed to surface during Tito's reign, causing major ethnic clashes. Yet prior to this situation Yugoslavia was deemed to have one of the best constitutions for a country with a diverse population, in that it addressed minority and other ethnic rights in sensitive ways. The personalised role of Tito as the supreme arbiter and his methods of managing disputes through political pressure in pre-arranged meetings, projected an image of Yugoslavia as a society without conflicts. When Tito died in 1980 and the party collapsed, conflicts started developing everywhere in the country with no democratic structures, institutions or procedures to manage and end them (Pajic, 1994). Although the experiences in Northern Ireland show that these are not always sufficient to quell ethnic disputes.

One common point emerges from the experiences of control over ethnically diverse populations in South Africa and Yugoslavia *i.e.* the preponderance of leaders with the ability to manage and control ethnic disputes. Neither the era of Mandela's statesmanship nor the human rights orientation of South Africa's constitution should be considered sufficient to steer the country away from future ethnic conflicts. Nor should the constitution be considered sufficient to create a sense of belonging to the country among its minorities when, in terms of the European definition of minority rights, it offers very little to them as segments of a population. For instance, the restoration of Indian languages and offering of more facilities such as through the electronic media by constitutional means and effective action, will constitute a strong symbolic message of their proper integration into the wider South African arena and is likely to impact upon future patterns of voting. But more importantly, a revision of the Bill of Rights and debate about the direction and implications of the CSCE on minority rights can help to produce a more appropriate constitution that is in line with important contemporary developments in other parts of the world. As it stands South Africa's present constitution is more a reflection of the demands of post-World War II conditions, based more on individual rights than on collective rights. This is not to imply that minority or ethnic rights should replace individual rights. I am of the conviction that there could be no respect and acceptance for ethnic or minority rights if there are no individual rights. It will be a realistic position to adopt since the very basis of the South African government's approach to reconstruction and development, and rightly so, is empathetically based along racial and ethnic lines as well. The fruition of racial equality is unlikely to be achieved in the near future. However, there appears to be a sort of undeclared but farcical thought that if racial equality is ever achieved, then ethnic differences are likely to dissipate. History has shown the difficulties of achieving either of these objectives. This suggestion should not be mistaken to be a tacit call for a return to the ethnic constitutionalism of the apartheid era. It is instead a call to debate these issues further in order to try and synchronise individual and minority rights in ways that would demonstrate a positive approach towards dealing with minority issues.

In order to acquire a more in-depth understanding of Indians perceptions of and responses to transformation, the issues discussed above must also be viewed against several conventional norms and world-views that they have carried across from India and which still persists. Among Indians, subscriptions to customary norms are central to life's values and in a creation of a general consciousness. Living in one house for as long as possible, monogamy, remaining married to one person and avoiding divorce, staying in one job for as long as possible, maintaining strong family values, among other issues, are signs of stability, orderliness and belief that such factors are the ways in which societies should function. Discipline and adherence to conventional norms is what is widely considered among Indians to produce stability and orderliness. Its effect is to produce positive perceptions and responses on an individual level and in civil society in general. Any deviation from this pattern is prone to be labelled as signs of instability, either in an individual's life or in society. It is for these reasons, together with the range of negative experiences since the 1994 general election, that the euphoria and optimism before and after April 1994 was so short lived.

BIBLIOGRAPHY

Allen, D.E. and Guy, R.F. (1978). *Conversation Analysis: The Sociology of Talk,* The Hague, Mouton.

Argyle, J. and Preston-Whyte E. (eds) (1978). *Social Systems and Tradition in South Africa*, Oxford, Oxford University Press.

Arkin A.J. *et al.* (1989). *The Indian South African: A Contemporary Profile,* Pinetown, Owen Burgess.

Bagwandeen D. (1989). "Historical Perspectives" in A.J. Arkin *et al.* (eds.), *The Indian South Africans,* Pinetown, South Africa, Owen Burgess Publishers.

Bayart J.F. (1993). *The State in Africa—The Politics of the Belly,* London, Longman.

Benedict A. [1991 (1983)]. *Imagined Communities—Reflections on the Origins and Spread of Nationalism,* 2nd edition. London, Verso.

Bhana S. and Brain J. (1990). *Setting Down Roots—Indian Immigrants in South Africa,* Johannesburg, Witwatersrand University Press.

Bhatia P. (1973). *Indian Ordeal in Africa,* Delhi: Vikas Publishing House Pvt. Ltd.

Blumer H. (1966). "Sociological implications of the thought of George Herbert Mead". *American Journal of Sociology*, 71:5:535-44.

Brass P. (1985) (ed). *Ethnic Groups and the State,* London, Croom Helm.

Breslin E.D. (1994). "U.S. Aid, the state and food insecurity in rural Zimbabwe: The case of Gokwe", *The Journal of Modern African Studies,* 32:1: 81-110.

Bugwandeen D. (1989). Historical Perspectives. In A.J. Arkin *et al.* (eds). *The Indian South Africans.* Pinetown: Owen Burgess Publishers.

Burgess R.G. (1984). *In the Field: An Introduction to Field Research,* London, George Allen and Unwin.

Byerley M. (1989). Mass Violence in Durban's Settlements in the 1980s, Unpublished M.Sc. Thesis, Department of Geographical Studies and Environmental Sciences, University of Natal, Durban.

Calpin G.H. (1949). *Indians in South Africa,* Pietermaritzburg, Shuter and Shuter.

Carmen R. (1996). *Autonomous Development—Humanising the Landscape: An Excursion Into Radical Thinking and Practice,* London, Zed Books.

Charney C. (1991). Vigilantes, Clientelism, and the South African State. *Transformation:* 16.

Cohen A. (1974). *Two Dimensional Man*, London, Tavistock.

Community Research Unit (1986). Socio-Economic Conditions and Household Subsistence Levels in four Durban Communities: Chatsworth, Newlands East, Phoenix and Wentworth. Unpublished Report.

Comrie M. (1985). "Interview with Mr. Sam Chetty", In *Natalia*: Volume 15:10-19.

Coopan S. (1948). *A Summary of the Education of the Indian in Natal, 1860-1947*—Ph.D. Dissertation, University of Cape Town.

Cumpston I.M. (1969). Indians Overseas, *British Territories, 1834—1854*, London, Dryden Press.

Davidson B. (1992). *The Black Man's Burden—Africa and the Curse of the Nation-State*, London, James Currey.

Desai A. (1999). *South Africa Still Revolting*, Johannesburg, Impact Africa Publishing Co.

Eriksen T.H. (1993). *Ethnicity and Nationalism: Anthropological Perspective*, London, Pluto Press.

Essop P. (1972). *The Development of Indian Political Movements in South Africa, 1924-1946.* PhD Dissertation, Sussex University.

Filatova I. (1997). "The Rainbow Against the African Sky or African Hegemony in a Multi-Cultural Context?", *Transformation*: 34:47-56.

Fortes M. (1958). "The Developmental Cycle of Domestic Groups." In Jack Goody (ed) *The Developmental Cycle in Domestic Groups*, Cambridge.

Frank A.G. (1969). *Capitalism and Underdevelopment in Latin America*, New York, Monthly Review Press.

Frederikse J. (1990). *The Unbreakable Thread: Non-Racialism in South Africa*, Johannesburg, Ravan Press.

Freund B. (1995). *Insiders and Outsiders: The Indian Working Class of Durban, 1910-1990.* Pietermaritzburg: University of Natal Press.

Gellner E. (1983). *Nations and Nationalism*, Oxford, Basil Blackwell.

Gellner E. (1987). *Culture, Identity and Politics*, Cambridge, Cambridge University Press.

Ginwala F. (1974). *Class Consciousness and Control—Indian South Africans, 1860-1946*, PhD Dissertation, Oxford University.

Glaser D. (1997). "South Africa and the limits of civil society", *Journal of Southern African Studies*, 23:1:5-25.

Good K. (1986). "Systematic agricultural mismanagement: The 1985 bumper harvest in Zambia." *The Journal of Modern African Studies*, 24:1: 257-284.

Good K. (1997). "Accountable to themselves: Predominance in Southern Africa". *The Journal of Modern African Studies*, 35:4:547-573.

Good K. (1999). "The State and Extreme Poverty in Botswana: The San and Destitutes". *The Journal of Modern African Studies*, 37:2:185-205.

Greenberg S. (1980). *Race and State in Capitalist Development—South Africa in Comparative Perspective*, Johannesburg. Ravan Press.

Greyling J. (1979). Land Ownership Patterns : A Case Study of the Natal North Coast. In B. Pachai (ed) *South Africa's Indians: The Evolution of a Minority,* University Press of America.

Griesman, B.E. (ed) (1975). *Minorities: A Text with Readings in Intergroup Relations,* Hinsdale, Illinois, The Dryden Press.

Hadden T. (1994). "Northern Ireland", In Hugh Miall (ed) *Minority Rights in Europe: The Scope for a Transnational Regime,* London, Pinter Publishers.

Hill P. (1986). *Development Economics on Trial: The Anthropological Case for a Prosecution.* Cambridge. Cambridge University Press.

Hindson D.C. and Byerly M.A. (1993). *Class and Residential Movement—Report on a Survey of Households in Canaan Squatter Camp,* Urban Studies Unit, Institute for Social and Economic Research, University of Durban-Westville.

Hindson D. *et al.* (1994). "From violence to reconstruction: The making, disintegration and remaking of an apartheid city", *Antipode—A Radical Journal of Geography,* 26: 4.

Hirschmann A.O. (1970). *Exit, Voice, Loyalty: Responses to Decline in Firms, Organisations and States,* Cambridge, Mass, Harvard University Press.

Hobsbawn E.G. (1990). *Nations and Nationalism since 1780s: Programme, Myth, Reality,* Cambridge, Cambridge University Press.

Horowitz D.L. (1991). *A Democratic South Africa? Constitutional Engineering in a Divided South Africa,* Cape Town, Oxford University Press.

Howe G. (1993). "The Ethnic Taboo" (editorial comment), *Indicator, South Africa,* 10:3:4.

Hughes S. (1987). Violence in Inanda, August 1985, *Journal of Southern Africa Studies* 13: 3.

Huntington S.P. (1968). *Political Order in Changing Societies,* New Haven and London, Yale University Press.

Hyden G. (1983). *No Shortcuts to Progress: African Development Management in Perspective,* London, Heineman.

Jain R.K. (1993). *Indian Communities Abroad: Themes and Literature,* New Delhi, Manohar Publishers and Distributors.

Jain R.K. (1994). "Civilisations and Settlement Societies: Cultural Development and Identity at the End of the Twentieth Century", *The Eastern Anthropologist,* 47 : 1 : 1-14.

Jithoo S. (1978). Complex Households and Joint Families Amongst Indians in Durban. In J. Argyle and E. Preston-Whyte (eds). *Social Systems and Tradition in South Africa,* Oxford University Press.

Jithoo S. (1985). "Indian Family Businesses in Durban, South Africa", in *Journal of Comparative Family Studies* XVI:3: 365-376.

Johnson R. (1973). *Indians and Apartheid in South Africa: The Failure of Resistance,* High Wycombe: University Microfilms Ltd.

Joshi P.S. (1942). *The Tyranny of Colour: A Study of the Indian People in South Africa,* Durban, E.P. and Commercial Printing Company Limited.

Keesing R.M. (1981). *Cultural Anthropology: A Contemporary Perspective,* New York, Holt, Rhinehart and Winston.

Khosa M. (1991). "Apartheid State and the Black Taxi Industry", Paper presented at the Conference of the Association of American Geographers, Miami, Florida. School of Geography, Oxford University.

Khosa M. (1992). "Changing state policy and the Black taxi industry in Soweto", In D.M. Smith (ed), *The Apartheid City and Beyond,* London, Routledge.

Klass M. (1961). *East Indians in Trinidad: A Study of Cultural Persistence.* New York, Columbia University Press.

Kuper H. (1956). "An ethnographic description of a Hindustani marriage in Durban", *African Studies,* 15:4:207-216.

Kuper H. (1957). "An interpretation of Hindu marriages in Durban". *African Studies,* 16:4:221-235.

Kuper H. (1960). *Indian People in Natal*, Durban, Natal University Press.

Kuper L. (1957). *Passive Resistance in South Africa,* New Haven, Yale University Press.

Kuper L. (1965). *An African Bourgeoisie: Race, Class and Politics in South Africa*, New Haven, Yale University Press.

Lee R. and Schlemmer L. (1991) (eds). *Transition to Democracy: Policy Perspectives 1991,* Cape Town, Oxford University Press.

Macdonald M. (1996). "Power Politics in the New South Africa". *Journal of Southern African Studies,* 22:2:221-233.

Makgetla N.S. (1986). "Theoretical and practical implications of IMF conditionality in Zambia". *The Journal of Modern African Studies,* 24:3: pp. 395-422.

Maharaj B. (1992). *The Group Areas Act in Durban: Central-Local State Relations,* PhD, Department of Geography, University of Natal, Pietermaritzburg.

Maharaj P. (1995). *The Social Identities of Indians in a Changing South Africa,* Master of Social Science Dissertation, Department of Sociology, University of Natal, Pietermaritzburg.

Makhatini M. (1999). "The Case of Cato Manor", in Doug Hindson and Jeff McCarthy (eds), *Here to Stay: Informal Settlements in KwaZulu-Natal,* Durban, Indicator Press, University of Natal.

Manganyi N.C. and Du Toit A. (eds) (1990). *Political Violence and the Struggle in South Africa*, London, Macmillan Press.

Mantzaris E.A. (1988). "Religion as a factor affecting the attitudes of South African Indians towards family solidarity and older persons", *South African Journal of Sociology,* 19:3: pp. 111-116.

Mare G. (1992). *Brothers Born of Warrior Blood: Politics and Ethnicity in South Africa,* Johannesburg, Ravan Press.

Martin W.G. and Beittel M. (1987). "The Hidden Abode of Reproduction: Conceptualizing Households in Southem Africa", in *Development and Change*:18: 2:215-234.

Mayall J. (1994). "Sovereignty and self-determination in the new Europe". In Hugh Miall (ed). *Minority Rights in Europe: The Scope for a Transnational Regime,* London, Pinter Publishers.

McCarthy J. and Hindson D. (eds) (1994). *Here to Stay—Informal Settlements in KwaZulu-Natal.* Durban, Indicator Press, University of Natal.

McCreedy W.C. (1983). *Culture, Ethnicity and Identity: Current Issues in Research*, New York, Heineman.

Meer F. (1969). *Portrait of South African Indians,* Durban, Avon Publishers.

Meer F. (1985). *Special Report: Unrest in Natal. August 1985,* Durban, Institute for Black Research, University of Natal.

Meer F. (ed.) (1991). *"Dr Yusuf Mohammed Dadoo: His Speeches, Articles and Correspondence with Mahatma Gandhi"*, Durban, Madiba Publishers.

Miall H. (1994). "Introduction", In Hugh Miall (ed) *Minority Rights in Europe: The Scope for a Transnational Regime,* London, Pinter Publishers.

Moodley K. (1989). "Cultural Politics" in A.J. Arkin (*et al.*) (eds), *The Indian South Africans: A Contemporary Perspective,* Pinetown, Owen Burgess Publishers.

Mukherji P.N. (1994). "The Indian State in Crisis? Nationalism and Nation Building", in *Sociological Bulletin—Journal of the Indian Sociological Society,* 42:1:21-50.

Mukherji S.B. (1959). *Indian Minority in South Africa,* New Delhi, People's Publishing House (Private) Ltd.

Muller A.L. (1968). *Minority Interests: The Political Economy of the Coloured and Indian Communities in South Africa,* Johannesburg, South African Institute of Race Relations.

Murray C. (1981). *Families Divided: The Impact of Migrant Labour in Lesotho,* Johannesburg, Ravan Press.

Murray C. (1987). "Class, Gender and the Household: The Developmental Cycle in Southern Africa", in *Development and Change,* 18:2:235-249.

Nanjira C.D. (1976). *The South Africa State in East Africa: Asians and Europeans in Tanzania, Uganda and Kenya,* Praeger Publishers.

Natal Indian Congress (*Founded by Mahatma Gandhi in 1894*), First statement on the Subject of Amenities and Housing presented to the Indian Penetration Commission, 2 April 1941.

Natal Indian Congress (*Founded by Mahatma Gandhi in 1894*), Memorandum on Housing, submitted to Natal Indian Judicial Commission, 1944.

Natal Indian Congress (*Founded by Mahatma Gandhi in 1894*), Fourth Annual Provincial Conference, 30 September-1 and 2 October 1950, held in the Madressa Anjuman Islam Hall, Durban.

Natal Indian Congress (*Founded by Mahatma Gandhi in 1894*), Tenth Annual Provincial Conference, 22, 23, 24 November 1957, Durban.

Natal Indian Congress (*Founded by Mahatma Gandhi in 1894*), Third and final memorandum submitted to the Indian Penetration Commission, 28 April 1941.

Nkwi P.N. (1997). "Rethinking the Role of Elites in Rural Development: A Case Study from Cameroon", *Journal of Contemporary African Studies*, 15:1:67-86.

Nuttal T. (1989). The Durban Riots of 1949 and the Struggle for the City, Unpublished Paper—Critical Perspectives on Southern Africa Seminar, University of Natal, Durban.

Olivier de Sardan J.P. (1999). "A moral economy of corruption in Africa", *The Journal of Modern African Studies*, 37:1:25-52.

Pachai B. (1979). Aliens in the Political Hierarchy in B. Pachai (ed) *South Africa's Indians: The Evolution of a Minority*. University Press of America.

Pahad E. (1972). *The Development of Indian Political Movements in South Africa, 1924-1946*, unpublished PhD Thesis, Sussex University.

Pajic Z. (1994). "The former Yugoslavia", In Hugh Miall (ed) *Minority Rights in Europe: The Scope for a Transnational Regime*, London, Pinter Publishers.

Palmer M. (1957). *The History of the Indian in Natal: Natal Regional Survey*, Vol. X, Cape Town, Oxford University Press.

Pather P.R. (1950). Seventy-years of Frustration and Unhappiness—An Examination of Land and Trading Rights as they affect Indians in Natal and the Transvaal and a criticism of the Group Areas Act 41: 1950, Durban, Mercantile Printing Press.

Raff C. (1996). *Autonomous Development: Humanising the Landscape*, London, Zed Books.

Rambiritch B. (n.d.). A brief overview of Indian education: 1860-1960, Unpublished Paper—Documentation Centre, University of Durban-Westville.

Ramphal R. (1989). "Social Transition" in A.J. Arkin *et al.* (eds), *The Indian South Africans: A Contemporary Perspective*, Pinetown, Owen Burgess.

Ramphal R. (1993). "Indians in a changing South Africa", in *Eastern Anthropologist*, 46:2:77-83.

Richburg K. (1997). *Out of America: A Black Man Confronts Africa*, New York, Basic Books.

Sannyasi B.D. and Chaturvedi B. (1931). *A Report on the Emigrants Repatriated to India under the Assisted Emigration Scheme from South Africa and on the Problem of Returned Emigrants from all Colonies.*

Saran P. (1985). *The Asian Indian Experience in the United States*, Cambridge, Ma, Schenman Books, Inc.

Schlemmer L. (1991). "The turn in the road: Emerging Conditions in 1990". In Robin and Lawrence Schlemmer (eds), *Transition to Democracy: Policy Perspective 1991*, Cape Town, Oxford University Press.

Schoombee G.F. and Mantzaris E (1986). "Attitudes of South African Indians towards westernisation and its effects on their family life: A pilot study", in *South African Journal of Sociology*, 17:1.

Sharma K.N. (n.d.). *Changing Forms of East Indian Marriage and Family in the Caribbean.* Mimeographed.

Sharp J.S. (1988). "Ethnic Groups and Nation: The Apartheid Vision in South Africa". In E. Boonzaier and J.S. Sharp (eds), *South African Keywords, Uses and Abuses in Political Concepts.*

Sharp J.S. and Spiegel A.D. (1985). "Vulnerability to Impoverishment in South African Rural Areas: The Erosion of Kinship and Neighbourhood as Social Resources," in *Africa,* 55:2:133-152.

Singh A. (1992). "The State, Ethnicity and Violence against Indians in South Africa," in *Eastern Anthropologist,* 45: 4: 341-363.

Singh A., Thorold A., Vawda S. (1997). *Living on the Edge: Squatters in the Durban Area, South Africa. Urban Working Research Papers: 43.* Department of Cultural Anthropology/Sociology of Development, Vrije Universiteit, Amsterdam. *Special Edition.*

Singh A. (1999). "The Constitution, Ethnicity and Minority Rights in Post-Apartheid South Africa", Paper presented at the South African Sociological Association Conference, Military Academy, Saldanha Bay, 6-9 July 1999.

Singh S.S. (1977). "Pioneers in passenger transport". In *Fiat Lux* (state sponsored magazine), August.

Sitas A. (1986). "Inanda 1985: Where Wealth and Power and Blood Reign Worshipped Gods", *South African Labour Bulletin,* 11:4: 85-119.

Sitas A. *et al.* (1995). "Where is the Labour Movement going to in KwaZulu-Natal?", *South African Labour Bulletin,* 19:6.

Sitas A. (1998). "South Africa in the 1990s: The logic of fragmentation and reconstruction". *Transformation,* 36:37-50.

Sooklal A. and Singh N. (1993). "The Erosion of Traditional Values: The Breakdown of the Joint Family and its Implications for the Hindu Community of South Africa", *International Journal on the Unity of the Sciences.*

Sparks A. (1994). *Tomorrow is Another Country: The Inside Story of South Africa's Negotiated Revolution,* Johannesburg, Struik.

Spiegel A.D. (1986). "Fluidity of Household Composition in Matatiele, Transkei: A Methodological Problem", in *Africa,* 45:I:17-35.

Supersad V. (1984). "Socio-economic Status of Selected Communities in the Durban Metropolitan Area", Paper for the Second Carnegie Inquiry into Poverty and Development in Southern Africa.

Swanson M.W. (1983). "The Asiatic Menace: Creating Segregation in Durban, 1870-1900", in *International Journal of African Historical Studies,* 16:401-421.

Thompson L. (ed) 1975. *Change in Contemporary South Africa—Perspectives on Southern Africa,* Berkely, University of California Press.

Thorold A. (1997). "The Politics of Mysticism: Sufism and Yao Identity in Southern Malawi", *Journal of Contemporary African Studies,* 15:1: p. 107-118.

Tinker H. (1976). *Separate and Unequal: India and the Indians in the British Commonwealth, 1920-1950,* London, C. Hurst.

Toli R. (1991). *The Origins of the Durban Strikes in 1973*, M.A. Thesis, University of Durban-Westville, South Africa.

Vahed G.H. (1995). *The Making of an Indian Identity in Durban, 1914-1949.* PhD Dissertation, Department of History, Indiana University, USA.

Van Den Berghe P.L. (1969). "Pluralism and polity: a theoretical explanation", in L. Kuper and M.G.Smith (eds), *Pluralism in Africa,* Berkely, University of California Press.

Venugopal L.N. (1993). "G.S. Gurye on Culture and Nation Building" in *Sociological Bulletin*: *Journal of the Indian Sociological Society*, 43:1:21-50.

Webster E. (1978). The 1949 Durban Riots—A Case Study in Race and Class. In P. Bonner (ed), *Working Papers in Southern African Studies,* Johannesburg: African Studies Institute.

Wilson F. and Ramphele M. (1989). *Uprooting Poverty, the South African Challenge, Report for the Second Carnegie Inquiry into Poverty and Development in Southern Africa,* South Africa, David Philip.

Wolpe H. (1988). *Race, Class and the Apartheid State,* London, James Curry.

Yudelman D. (1977). *From Faire to International State: Subjugation and Co-operation of Organized Labour on the South African Gold Mines, 1902-1930,* London, University Microfilm International.

Index